CHRISTA WATSON

PIECE AND QUILT
with PRECUTS

11 Quilts ▪ **18** Machine-Quilting Designs ▪ *Start-to-Finish Success!*

Martingale
Create with Confidence

Piece and Quilt with Precuts:
11 Quilts, 18 Machine-Quilting Designs, Start-to-Finish Success!
© 2017 by Christa Watson

Martingale®
19021 120th Ave. NE, Ste. 102
Bothell, WA 98011-9511 USA
ShopMartingale.com

Printed in China
22 21 20 19 18 17   8 7 6 5 4 3 2 1

Library of Congress Cataloging-in-Publication Data
is available upon request.

ISBN: 978-1-60468-870-2

MISSION STATEMENT

We empower makers who use fabric and yarn
to make life more enjoyable.

CREDITS

**PUBLISHER AND
CHIEF VISIONARY OFFICER**
Jennifer Erbe Keltner

CONTENT DIRECTOR
Karen Costello Soltys

DESIGN MANAGER
Adrienne Smitke

MANAGING EDITOR
Tina Cook

PRODUCTION MANAGER
Regina Girard

ACQUISITIONS EDITOR
Karen M. Burns

PHOTOGRAPHER
Brent Kane

TECHNICAL EDITOR
Nancy Mahoney

ILLUSTRATOR
Sandy Huffaker

COPY EDITOR
Durby Peterson

DEDICATION

*To my parents—thanks to you, Mom, for supporting
my artistic endeavors at a young age, and to you,
Dad, for always encouraging my entrepreneurial spirit.*

CONTENTS

INTRODUCTION

Thank you for reading this book! I'm so grateful for the tremendous response to my previous two books, Machine Quilting with Style *(Martingale, 2015) and* The Ultimate Guide to Machine Quilting *(coauthored with Angela Walters, Martingale, 2016). I'm excited to be back with more fun ideas for you to try. It makes my heart happy to know that so many of you enjoy the quiltmaking process as much as I do.*

In Piece and Quilt with Precuts, *I focus on piecing with precut strips and squares along with conveniently packaged fabric bundles and leftover precuts (or scraps) from other projects. Working with precuts allows me to finish quilt tops more quickly so I can get to my favorite part of the process—machine quilting! Whether you enjoy quilting by hand or by machine or even "by check," the pieced patterns and machine quilting motifs presented here are sure to inspire you every step of the way.*

The quilts are presented in three categories so you can easily build your machine quilting skills. The first group uses walking-foot quilting exclusively, to get you comfortable with the machine-quilting process. The next group features free-motion designs that will inspire confidence. The last group combines both techniques to bring it all together. I encourage you to mix and match the motifs for even more possibilities, and to remember that finished is better than perfect.

~ Christa

WORKING WITH PRECUTS

I love working with precuts because they can be incorporated into practically any quilt design. In this section, you'll find tips on working with precuts to get the most out of these beautiful, colorful bundles.

What Are Precuts?

Precuts are small- to medium-sized pieces of fabric cut into specific shapes and sizes, usually by a fabric manufacturer. A package of precuts contains one or more same-sized pieces from an entire fabric collection. The convenient bundles are known by various names, depending on the fabric manufacturer and size of the precut. Since the number of individual units in a precut bundle can vary widely, the materials list for each project in this book indicates the number of specific precut pieces required, rather than the number of precut bundles.

Precut sizes can vary slightly from one fabric manufacturer to the next. Be sure to measure the length and width of the piece to see if the stated size includes the pinked edges of the fabric. Usually a manufacturer will be consistent with sizing across collections, so it may be easier to stick with one fabric brand if you're worried about consistency. If precut sizes vary, you can either trim all the precuts down to the same size or use the edge of the correctly sized piece as a guide when piecing.

There are almost as many different types of precuts as there are fabric brands. If you need a particular fabric piece and it's not available, consider using the next larger size and trimming it to the size you need. Or cut strips and squares from yardage or scraps.

In this book, the precut sizes I used are as follows:

- 2½" squares
- 5" squares
- 10" squares
- 1½"-wide strips
- 2½"-wide strips
- 3½"-wide strips
- Fat eighths (9" × 21")
- Fat quarters (18" × 21")

Most, if not all, of your favorite fabric companies offer some sort of precut. They change the lineups from time to time, so check your favorite quilt shop or online at ThePrecutStore.com to find the sizes, colors, and prints you want to use.

Choosing Fabrics

Working with precut bundles simplifies the task of selecting fabrics for your quilts. The solids and prints in any group coordinate beautifully, and you'll automatically gain color confidence the more you use them.

NO NEED TO PREWASH

Prewashing is not recommended with precuts other than fat quarters. Because smaller pieces can warp, a safer bet is to wash the finished quilt when complete, using dye-magnet sheets (such as Shout Color Catchers) to catch excess dye in the wash. I haven't had any problems with shrinkage when mixing washed and unwashed fabrics in the same quilt.

CONTRAST IS KEY

The easiest way to choose precuts for a quilt is to pair prints or focus fabrics with a contrasting light or dark background. Neutrals, such as white or black, work like a charm, but you can also think outside the box. Colors can work just as well as black or white for quilt backgrounds. To create sharp definition between the blocks, choose a background fabric that contrasts well with every other fabric in the bundle. When making a scrappy quilt, a variety of light (also known as *low-volume*) prints can showcase the colorful scraps.

Remember that there are two sides to every fabric! If you need more contrast, consider using the *wrong side* of a fabric in the background. For some quilts, I used the wrong side of many fabrics to create more contrast between the background and the blocks.

I used the "wrong" side of many precut scraps in the background of Spools (above and on page 89) to create more contrast. They were just right for this quilt!

CURATE A COLLECTION

When fabric designers use a defined color palette, it's easy to mix and match among their collections in one quilt. You can easily substitute fabric from a designer's newest line to replace older fabric that's out of print. If you have an older bundle that doesn't have enough pieces for the quilt you want to make, try mixing fabrics from older and newer lines to get the pieces you need, or throw in a few pieces from your stash to round out a collection.

It's also fun to mix fabrics from different designers. You can take apart precut bundles to create a unique bundle. You can also make your own precuts from your stash, using leftovers as a starting point to build a custom palette.

Speedy Sewing

Because I piece and quilt all of my own quilts, speedy sewing is a must in order for me to get it all done. Here are a few methods I use to work quickly and efficiently, while still maintaining accuracy.

STAY ORGANIZED

When sewing an entire stack of blocks, take a picture to act as a virtual design wall when you're sewing the blocks together. Stack up as many similar units or blocks as you can next to your sewing machine, so you can sew continuously without having to get up and move the units around. Even if you have only a few minutes a day to sew, keeping your blocks organized and ready to sew will allow you to get a lot done in stolen chunks of time throughout your day.

CHAIN PIECING

Look for areas of the design in which you can assembly-line sew the units to make the job go faster. To chain piece, start sewing on a small scrap of fabric (called a *leader*) to catch your beginning threads and prevent them from tangling or jamming your sewing machine.

Add the first pair of units under the machine, and keep sewing a few stitches beyond the first seam. Do not clip the threads. Instead, add the next pair and continue in the same manner until you have sewn as many units as possible. End with another scrap of fabric (called an *ender*) before you take the chain-pieced units off your machine. Then clip the threads between all of the units and assembly-line press.

I recommend making one test block first before massively chain piecing everything else. If you use scraps for the test block, you can save it for machine-quilting practice later on.

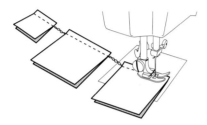

PINS ARE YOUR FRIENDS!

Contrary to popular belief, pinning generously doesn't actually slow down the work. If you follow the assembly-line method and pin each stack of units as you sew, you can breeze through block assembly in no time—and your blocks will be more precise. This will also reduce the chance you'll need to do the "frog stitch," otherwise known as "rip-it, rip-it!"

PRESSING MATTERS

I prefer to press my seam allowances open. In the long run, it saves time because I don't have to think about which way to press them. Any seam can easily be matched up with any other seam by adding a pin to either side of the seam intersections. To prevent seams from popping open, reduce the stitch length when piecing, or backstitch each unit before adding the next piece when chain piecing.

Pressing seam allowances open is especially helpful when machine quilting on a home sewing machine, because it allows the blocks and quilt top to lie extremely flat and eliminates many of the lumps and bumps that can break or damage the needle. The base of the machine provides stability while quilting, so nothing is pulling on the seams, even when stitching in the ditch.

Pressing seam allowances open also eliminates shadowing—the effect that happens when a dark fabric shows up underneath a lighter one. However, if you prefer to press seam allowances to one side, that's perfectly fine. Do what works best for you!

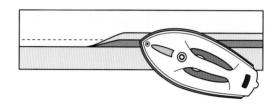

CUT, AND THEN SEW

After making numerous quilts, I've found that cutting each piece to size first and then sewing is actually faster and more accurate than strip piecing. When cutting individual pieces, you can layer several fabrics on top of each other and cut them all at once. Your pieces will also stay true to size. When strip piecing, it's hard to cut through more than one pieced unit at a time.

By working with shorter units rather than long strips, you'll reduce the risk of stretching your fabrics while sewing. You'll still benefit from speedy chain piecing, as mentioned on page 7, but cutting first ensures efficiency by allowing you to cut multiple-sized pieces from the same precut unit.

Not Enough Fabric

In each project, I've listed how many of each cut shape you'll need. When working with precuts, there usually isn't much waste, so be sure to cut carefully.

If you accidentally miscut and there isn't enough fabric to finish your quilt top as originally planned, go for a scrappy look and embrace this "happy accident" as a design opportunity!

HOW DO I QUILT IT?

The question I'm asked most often when I'm teaching is, "How do I quilt it?" The simple answer is, any way you like! But let's dive deeper and consider these important factors: Will it be an heirloom or show quilt? A functional quilt? A charity quilt or other gift from the heart? Also, how much time do you have to spend on the piece? What's your confidence level in attempting the design you wish to create? All of these factors will help shape your answer.

Make the Most of Your Time

If I'm making a quilt to enter into a quilt show, I'll spend much more time paying attention to details than I would if making a quick quilt for a friend's baby shower. For a show quilt, I quilt every inch, tie off every knot, and more often than not, take out any mistakes or wobbles. I usually quilt intricate designs that I'm familiar with and can execute well. I allow plenty of time so I don't feel rushed.

If I'm making a quilt that's meant to be loved and used, I'll choose a motif or two that I can quilt quickly. Or I might try out a new design. I know the recipient will love whatever I choose, so picking the "perfect" quilting pattern isn't a concern. Of course in either scenario, I'll still have fun and enjoy the process!

Consider Your Materials

If you're like me, you can't resist a great print! Busy fabrics are great for practicing your machine quilting, because they can hide mistakes. But once you've built up your confidence and are ready to show off your machine-quilting skills, you may want to opt for more solid or tonal groupings that will allow your quilting to really shine. Show off more intricate quilting motifs in high-contrast areas of the quilt, and save the low-contrast or busy areas for easy allover designs.

Although I enjoy piecing, I usually spend more time machine quilting than I spend sewing the top. Therefore I like to work with materials that are no-fuss and give me excellent results every time. I love working with premium quilting cottons and natural fiber battings like cotton or wool.

Dense cotton battings, like Warm and Natural, Hobbs, or Quilters Dream, are flat and easy to quilt through. The batting clings nicely to the fabric and will shrink a little when you wash the quilt, providing a cozy crinkly look that helps hide imperfections. Wool is loftier than cotton, so it provides good stitch definition. Wool is also lighter weight than cotton and doesn't hold wrinkles, so it's a good choice for show quilts, or quilts that will be folded and shipped.

Successful basting can make or break your quilt, so if you take the time to baste properly, the machine-quilting process will be much more fun! I baste my quilts using one of two methods—safety pins or basting spray. Safety pins are more economical but require a lot of pinning and unpinning, especially if the layers of the quilt shift and need to be repositioned. Using basting spray is faster but requires you to spray outside or in a well-ventilated room. You can find many tips on how to baste your quilts in my first book, *Machine Quilting with Style*, or at ShopMartingale.com/HowtoQuilt. I also have step-by-step photo tutorials for both methods at ChristaQuilts.com/tutorials.

The threads I use most often are available in my Piece and Quilt Collection from Aurifil, 50-weight cotton in both neutrals and colors.

Try Different Threads

Before you invest in a large thread stash, test different weights, colors, and brands to see what you and your machine prefer. After years of experimenting, I've decided that I like to keep things simple. Although I have a variety of colors in my thread stash, I prefer using one type of thread for both piecing and machine quilting.

My favorite thread is Aurifil 50-weight, 100% cotton. It's the perfect weight for piecing. It blends well and sinks into most fabrics when machine quilting, and it virtually disappears into the fabric when hand binding. By sticking to one type of thread, I usually have what I need on hand as soon as I'm ready to quilt. Plus, I don't have to store *all* the colors in *all* the different weights and fibers. As a bonus, I can use any thread left over in the bobbin when piecing my next scrappy quilt. I use size 80/12 needles (Sharp or Topstitch) for both piecing and machine quilting.

I try to match threads to my fabrics, and I always use the same thread color in the top and bobbin so that if there are any tension issues, they'll be less noticeable. Audition thread colors before quilting by unwrapping a few inches of thread from the spool and laying it across several different fabrics on the quilt top. Then pick whichever color blends the best. When in doubt, go with a slightly lighter thread color, especially on multicolored quilts. I think lighter thread on darker fabric looks much nicer than darker thread on lighter fabric.

Tan thread blends well with light and dark fabrics in Starstruck (above and on page 43).

Choose the Right Machine

While you can successfully quilt on any sewing machine, you can upgrade as you discover which features are important to you. "My Favorite Machine Features," right, lists those that make the job easier.

My machine of choice is a Bernina 770 Quilter's Edition.

No-Mark Quilting

To quilt quickly, embrace no-mark techniques. For walking-foot quilting, try quilting along seamlines and using the edge of the presser foot as a spacing guide. Walking-foot quilting works best when you're stitching long, straight lines. You'll need to rotate the quilt whenever the line changes direction, so choose designs with minimal movement. If the drag of the quilt causes the stitches to shrink, compensate by increasing the stitch length on your machine.

For no-mark free-motion quilting, choose small- to medium-scale asymmetrical textures that flow in any direction. Think of it as doodling on your quilt. Lower or cover the feed dogs so that you're moving freely.

Divide and Conquer

To "anchor" the quilt, first stitch large sections in the ditch, around blocks or rows. Then add more detailed quilting in smaller sections. Look for obvious design breaks where you can combine motifs. For example, you might quilt one motif in the blocks and a contrasting motif in the background between blocks.

MY FAVORITE MACHINE FEATURES

- Extended throat space (also known as *harp space*) between the needle and right edge of the machine. The standard width is approximately 6". Newer models of domestic machines can have up to 11" of space.

- A hands-free system or knee lift, which allows you to lift the presser foot so you can rotate the quilt with both hands.

- A hover setting that can easily be turned on and off—the foot will raise slightly as soon as you stop stitching, which makes it much easier to pivot the quilt.

- A built-in dual-feed system. This works similar to a walking foot, feeding all layers through the machine at the same time. It allows you to use a wider range of presser feet in the machine-quilting process.

- Open-toe feet so you can see the needle more clearly.

- Feet that can be easily switched, with nothing to screw or unscrew. This handy feature makes it easier to change feet when switching back and forth between free-motion quilting and walking-foot quilting.

- A variety of interesting decorative stitches that allow you to quilt more than simple, straight lines with the walking foot or dual-feed system. (Note: Throughout this book, the term *walking-foot quilting* refers to an attached walking foot as well as a dual-feed system.)

- A way to reduce the presser-foot pressure. When using a walking foot to quilt intersecting straight lines, I lower the pressure, which helps prevent puckers. But I use the default foot pressure when I'm free-motion quilting.

Try to start and end the quilting off the quilt, in the batting, or choose designs that can be quilted continuously from edge to edge. If you need to start or end a line of quilting in the middle of the quilt, try to backtrack over a previous line of stitching or stop in a seam if possible. See "Tying Off the Thread" below or start and end each line of quilting with a series of six to eight tiny stitches.

Manage the Bulk

Start quilting from the right edge of the quilt with the bulk to your left. Scrunch and smoosh the quilt out of the way as often as you can. When you reach the midpoint of the quilt, rotate it 180° and continue working from the center to the other edge of the quilt.

Each quilt that follows includes a quilting plan to help you manage the bulk and quilt efficiently.

TYING OFF THE THREAD

Quilt off the edge periodically to check your bobbin level. If you pay attention to how much area you can cover with one bobbin (such as several blocks), you can anticipate when your bobbin will run out and avoid having to change bobbins in the middle of the quilt.

If your quilt design starts or stops somewhere in the middle of the quilt, or if you run out of bobbin thread while quilting, you may need to tie off your loose ends. Start by bringing the bobbin thread to the top of the quilt by manually turning the hand wheel on your machine toward you to create one stitch (photo 1). Tug on the top thread to the pull the bobbin thread up to the top of the quilt (photo 2). Leaving several inches of thread,

continue stitching. When you're done stitching, tie a knot with both ends of thread. Use a self-threading needle to insert both threads into the quilt through the top and middle layer only. Pull the needle through to the top and clip off the excess thread, popping the knot through the quilt top and hiding it in the batting.

To bring up the bobbin thread at the end of a line of stitching, manually take a stitch and then pull your quilt a few inches away from the machine to create slack in the bobbin. Clip the thread from the underside of the quilt, leaving several inches. Use a pin to pull it through to the top. Make a knot, and pop it into the batting as before.

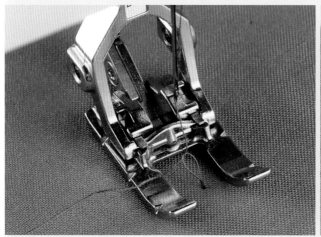

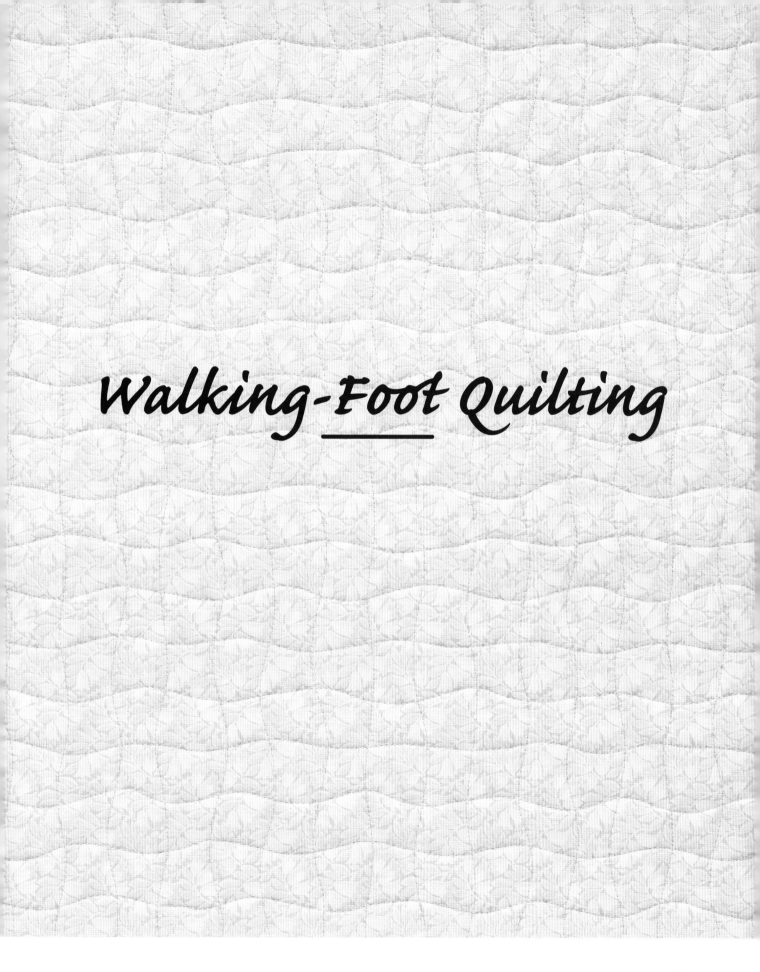

Walking-Foot Quilting

SQUIGGLES

Showcase a favorite fabric collection with this simple-to-piece design. Use your walking foot to add a layer of squiggly texture, and remember—it's okay to quilt outside the lines.

QUILT DETAILS

- Finished quilt: 50" × 63½"
- Finished block: 4½" × 9"
- Number of blocks: 77
- Batting: Quilters Dream Poly, Deluxe loft
- Quilting thread: Aurifil 50-weight in Aluminum
- Quilting designs: see "Quilting Squiggle Lines" on page 19

Materials

Yardage is based on 42"-wide fabric unless otherwise noted.

77 squares, 5" × 5" (*OR* 20 strips, 2½" × 42") of cream solid for background

39 squares, 10" × 10" (*OR* 154 squares, 5" × 5") of assorted prints for blocks

½ yard of blue print for binding

3¼ yards of fabric for backing

56" × 70" piece of batting

Approximately 1,200 yards of cotton thread for machine quilting

Cutting

From the cream solid squares or strips, cut a *total* of:
308 squares, 2½" × 2½"

From *each* of the assorted print 10" squares, cut:
4 squares, 5" × 5" (156 total; 2 are extra)

From the blue print, cut:
6 strips, 2¼" × 42"

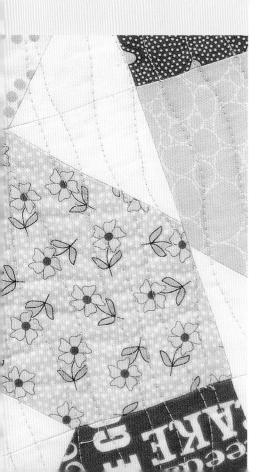

Squiggles is made using two Charm Packs (5" squares) of Bella Solids Porcelain and one Layer Cake (10" squares) of The Sweet Life by Pat Sloan, both by Moda Fabrics.

Making the Blocks

Press all seam allowances open, as indicated by the arrows.

1 Place two cream 2½" squares on opposite corners of a print 5" square. Draw a diagonal line from corner to corner across each cream square. Stitch on the drawn line. Trim away the corner fabric, leaving a ¼" seam allowance. (See "Bonus Units" on page 17 if you'd like to use the excess triangles in another project.) Flip the cream triangles open and press. The unit should measure 5" square, including the seam allowances. Make a total of 154 units.

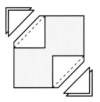

Make 154 units,
5" × 5".

BONUS UNITS

After marking the diagonal line on the cream 2½" squares, draw a second line ½" from the first line. Sew on both marked lines, and then cut between the two stitched lines. Press the seam allowances open. You'll have a block unit for this quilt and two bonus half-square-triangle units for another project. Trim the half-square-triangle units to measure 1¾" square. Use the half-square-triangle units and scraps to make Baby Geese, a bonus project online at ShopMartingale.com/Extras.

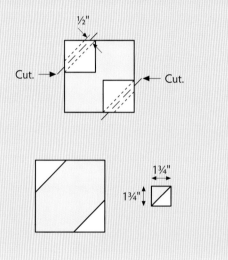

2 Randomly join two units to make a block measuring 5" × 9½", including the seam allowances, rotating one of the units to form a C shape. Make a total of 77 blocks.

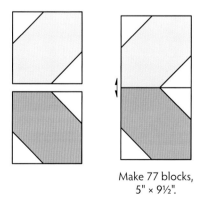

Make 77 blocks, 5" × 9½".

MATCHY MATCHY

If you're worried about matching up the center seam on the block, first sew large basting stitches for all the seam intersections. Inspect the seam and if you're satisfied, resew the entire seam using a regular stitch length.

Assembling the Quilt Top

1 Refer to the quilt assembly diagram on page 18 to randomly arrange the blocks in seven rows of 11 blocks each.

2 Sew the blocks together into rows. Note that when the blocks are joined, the cream triangle tips will not be aligned.

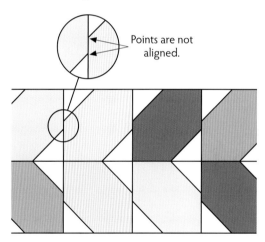

Points are not aligned.

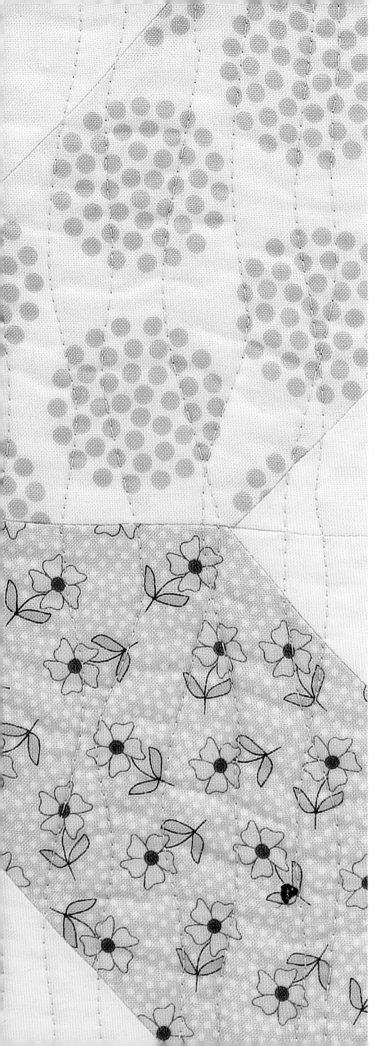

3 Join the rows to complete the quilt top. The quilt top should measure 50" × 63½", including the seam allowances.

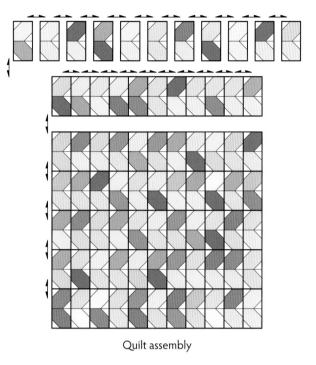

Quilt assembly

4 Stitch ⅛" from the edges on all four sides to prevent the edge seams from splitting open.

Finishing

You can find more information on piecing the backing, layering, basting, and binding your quilt at ShopMartingale.com/HowtoQuilt. Or for my particular methods, see *Machine Quilting with Style*.

1 Cut the backing yardage into two equal lengths and sew them together to make a backing approximately 6" longer and 6" wider than the quilt top.

2 Layer and baste the quilt using your favorite method.

3 Using a walking foot, quilt squiggle lines as described in "Quilting Squiggle Lines," opposite.

4 Trim the batting and backing flush with the quilt-top edges. Join the blue 2¼"-wide strips end to end to make one long strip. Bind the quilt edges by hand or machine using the pieced strip.

Quilting Squiggle Lines

Light gray or taupe thread blends well with most multicolored prints while still looking good on a lighter background fabric. One line of quilting will really stand out, but several lines can blend together to create an overall texture that's quite fast and easy to quilt.

1 Starting off the edge of the quilt, stitch a slightly wavy line next to each long vertical seamline, working your way across the quilt and following lines 1–5 on the quilting plan **(fig. 1)**. To create each squiggle, gently move the quilt from side to side as you stitch. When you reach the center, rotate the quilt 180°. Working from the center toward one side, quilt anchor lines 6–10 to secure the quilt.

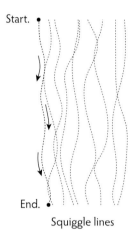

Squiggle lines

2 Fill in the rest of the quilt with additional squiggles by stitching random, slightly overlapping lines **(fig. 2)**. Quilt two or three squiggles per vertical row for a lighter amount of quilting; quilt more lines for a denser, more textured look.

FIG. 1

FIG. 2

Quilting plan

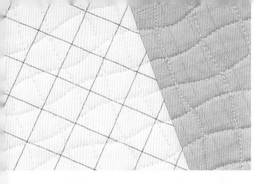

GRIDWORK

QUILT DETAILS

- Finished quilt: 54½" × 63½"
- Finished block: 9" × 9"
- Number of blocks: 42
- Batting: Pellon Nature's Touch Soy Blend, 50% soy/50% cotton
- Quilting thread: Aurifil 50-weight in Light Grey Blue
- Quilting designs: see "Quilting a Wavy Grid" on page 26

Add some whimsy to a traditional grid layout with funky, chunky blocks and "perfectly imperfect" wavy-grid quilting.

Materials

Yardage is based on 42"-wide fabric unless otherwise noted.

42 squares, 10" × 10", of assorted prints for blocks

42 squares, 5" × 5", of assorted solids for blocks

½ yard of tan solid for binding

3½ yards of fabric for backing

61" × 70" piece of batting

Approximately 1,200 yards of cotton thread for machine quilting

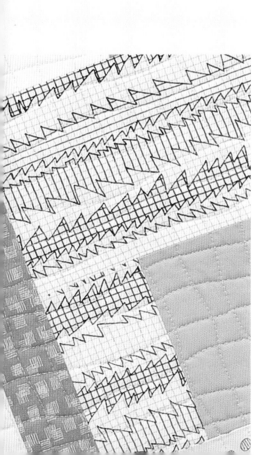

MAKE IT YOUR OWN

Contrast is key between the two precut collections—think solids versus prints, lights versus darks, and so on. For a different look, swap the placement of the solids and prints, or randomly vary the position of the smaller squares within each block. Another way to make it your own is to quilt straight lines instead of wavy lines. Use a guide bar attached to the walking foot to quilt a straight line grid and vary the spacing between the lines as desired.

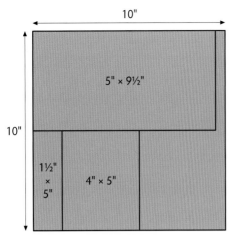

Cutting for group 1, blocks A and B.
Cut 14.

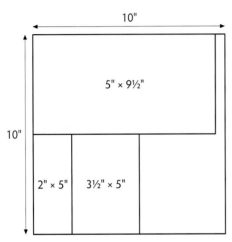

Cutting for group 2, blocks C and D.
Cut 14.

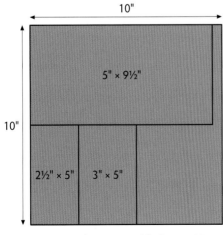

Cutting for group 3, blocks E and F.
Cut 14.

Cutting

Divide the 10" squares into three groups of 14 squares each. Group 1 will be for blocks A and B, group 2 for blocks C and D, and group 3 for blocks E and F. See the appropriate cutting diagram for each group.

From *each* of the squares in group 1, cut:
1 rectangle, 5" × 9½" (14 total)
1 rectangle, 1½" × 5" (14 total)
1 rectangle, 4" × 5" (14 total)

From *each* of the squares in group 2, cut:
1 rectangle, 5" × 9½" (14 total)
1 rectangle, 2" × 5" (14 total)
1 rectangle, 3½" × 5" (14 total)

From *each* of the squares in group 3, cut:
1 rectangle, 5" × 9½" (14 total)
1 rectangle, 2½" × 5" (14 total)
1 rectangle, 3" × 5" (14 total)

From the tan solid, cut:
7 strips, 2¼" × 42"

EFFICIENT CUTTING

When cutting the same-sized pieces, you can speed up the cutting process by stacking four squares and cutting them all at once. If working with precuts that are not exactly the same size, align two edges on the squares (such as the bottom and left edges), and then measure from the aligned edges to cut the required pieces.

Making Blocks A and B

Press all seam allowances open, as indicated by the arrows.

1 From the same print, lay out one 5" × 9½", one 1½" × 5", and one 4" × 5" rectangle. Add a contrasting solid 5" square. Sew the shorter

Gridwork is made using one pack of Ten Squares (10" squares) of Doe by Carolyn Friedlander and one pack of Charm Squares (5" squares) of Kona Solid Doe coordinates, both from Robert Kaufman Fabrics.

rectangles to opposite sides of the solid square. Sew the longer rectangle to the top of the unit to complete the block. The block should measure 9½" square, including the seam allowances. Make a total of seven A blocks.

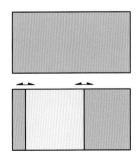
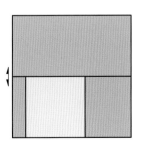

Block A.
Make 7 blocks, 9½" × 9½".

2 Repeat step 1, reversing the placement of the shorter rectangles to make seven B blocks measuring 9½" square, including the seam allowances.

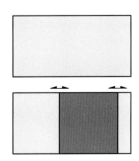
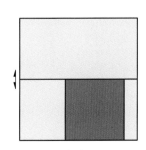

Block B.
Make 7 blocks, 9½" × 9½".

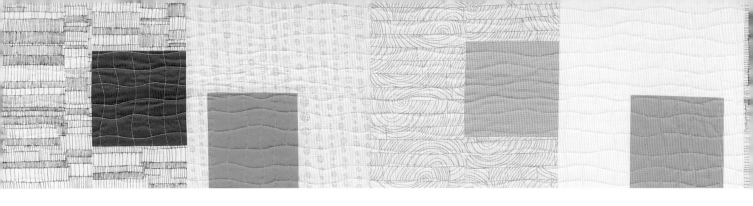

Making Blocks C and D

1 From the same print, lay out one 5" × 9½", one 2" × 5", and one 3½" × 5" rectangle. Add a contrasting solid 5" square. Sew the shorter rectangles to opposite sides of the solid square. Sew the longer rectangle to the top of the unit to complete the block. The block should measure 9½" square, including the seam allowances. Make a total of seven C blocks.

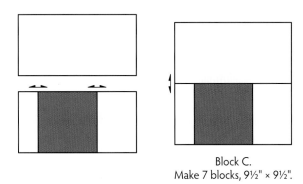

Block C.
Make 7 blocks, 9½" × 9½".

2 Repeat step 1, reversing the placement of the shorter rectangles to create seven D blocks measuring 9½" square, including the seam allowances.

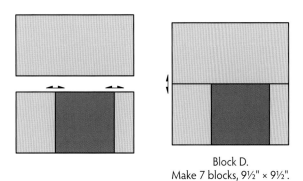

Block D.
Make 7 blocks, 9½" × 9½".

Making Blocks E and F

1 From the same print, lay out one 5" × 9½", one 2½" × 5", and one 3" × 5" rectangle. Add a contrasting solid 5" square. Sew the shorter rectangles to opposite sides of the solid square. Sew the longer rectangle to the top of the unit to complete the block. The block should measure 9½" square, including the seam allowances. Make a total of seven E blocks.

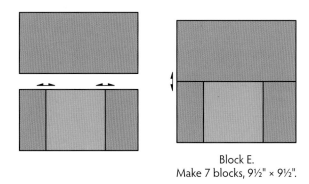

Block E.
Make 7 blocks, 9½" × 9½".

2 Repeat step 1, reversing the placement of the shorter rectangles to create seven F blocks measuring 9½" square, including the seam allowances.

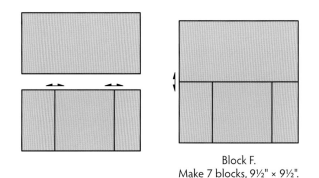

Block F.
Make 7 blocks, 9½" × 9½".

Set aside some of the leftover pieces to use in Spools on page 89. Or save them for another project.

Assembling the Quilt Top

1 Refer to the quilt assembly diagram below to arrange the blocks in seven rows of six blocks each. Vary the position and rotation of each block for a pleasing effect.

2 Sew the blocks together into rows. Join the rows to complete the quilt top. The top should measure 54½" × 63½", including the seam allowances.

3 Stitch ⅛" from the edges on all four sides to prevent the edge seams from splitting open.

Finishing

You can find more information on piecing the backing, layering, basting, and binding your quilt at ShopMartingale.com/HowtoQuilt. Or for my particular methods, see *Machine Quilting with Style*.

1 Cut the backing yardage into two equal lengths and sew them together to make a backing approximately 6" longer and 6" wider than the quilt top.

2 Layer and baste the quilt using your favorite method.

3 Using a walking foot, quilt a wavy grid as described in "Quilting a Wavy Grid" on page 26.

4 Trim the batting and backing flush with the quilt-top edges. Join the tan 2¼"-wide strips end to end to make one long strip. Bind the quilt edges by hand or machine using the pieced strip.

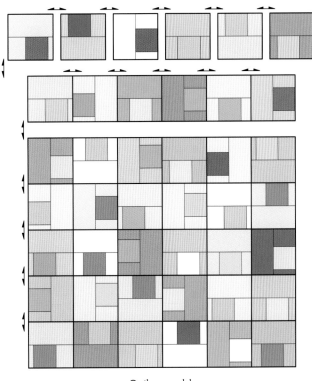

Quilt assembly

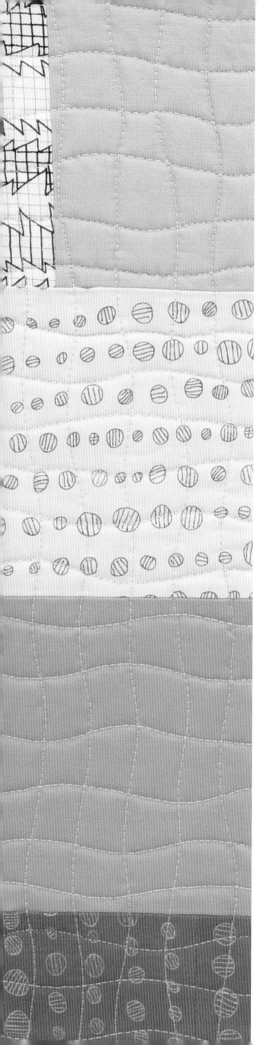

Quilting a Wavy Grid

When quilting intersecting lines with a walking foot, try to avoid the "snowplow" effect that happens when fabric is pushed across the quilt, causing it to pile up and pucker when you quilt perpendicular lines such as a grid. Quilt with a light hand and let the machine do most of the work while you gently ease the quilt through the machine. If it's an option on your machine, reduce the presser foot pressure to avoid puckers. If desired, sew on a scrap first to make sure your walking foot is working properly. To minimize the number of times you change directions while quilting, you'll only need to rotate the quilt once in each direction when you reach the center.

1 Quilt wavy lines similar to squiggles quilting on page 19. Starting off the edge of the quilt, stitch a vertical anchor line between all vertical rows of blocks, and another line through the center of each block. For a cleaner look, use the edge of your presser foot as a guide to stitch next to the seam, rather than crossing over the ditch. Work your way across the quilt following lines 1–6 on the quilting plan (fig. 1), opposite. When you reach the center, rotate the quilt 180°. Working from the center to the side, quilt anchor lines 7–11 to secure the quilt.

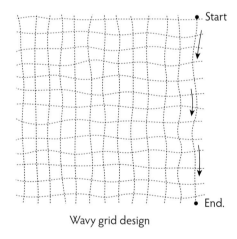

Wavy grid design

2 Rotate the quilt 90° and quilt horizontal anchor lines 12–24 in the same manner. The waves will appear larger or smaller depending on how much you turn the quilt while quilting. Use a piece of painter's tape as a guideline if needed to mark the center of your blocks, or just randomly eyeball it for a more whimsical look.

3 Quilt another line roughly halfway between the two previously quilted lines. Keep going, quilting one set of lines completely across the quilt in both directions to create a smaller and smaller grid until you're happy with the spacing. The quilting plan on page 27 shows six lines per block in each direction. However, I quilted lines approximately ¾" to 1" apart, with about 12 lines per block in each direction (fig. 2).

FIG. 1

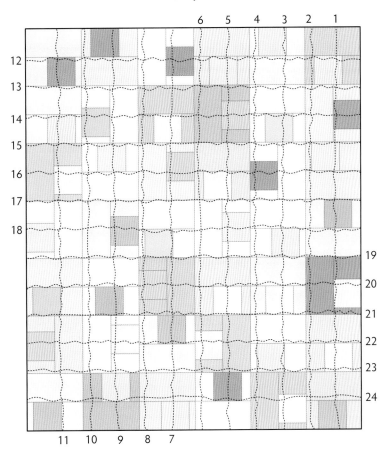

FIG. 2

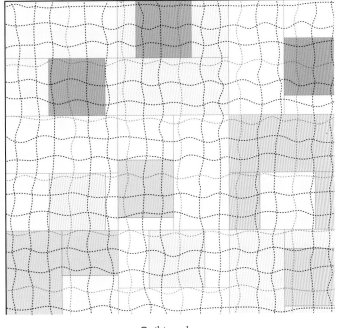

Quilting plan

FREQUENCY

QUILT DETAILS

- Finished quilt: 54½" × 54½"
- Finished block: 18" × 18"
- Number of blocks: 9
- Batting: Warm and Natural Cotton
- Quilting thread: Aurifil 50-weight in Bamboo
- Quilting designs: see "Quilting Modern Zigzags" on page 32

Combine a bit of structured improv piecing with a dash of modern machine quilting for a truly unique creation, proving that you can indeed make a modern quilt from precuts!

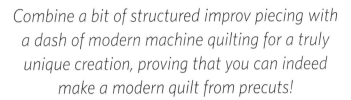

Materials

Yardage is based on 42"-wide fabric unless otherwise noted.

20 strips, 2½" × 42", of assorted light batiks for block background

40 strips, 2½" × 42", of assorted medium to dark batiks for blocks (referred to collectively as "dark")

½ yard of teal print for binding

3½ yards of fabric for backing

61" × 61" square of batting

Approximately 1,200 yards of cotton thread for machine quilting

Cutting

From the light batik strips, cut:
80 rectangles, 2½" × 10"

From the dark batik strips, cut:
1 strip, 2½" × 42"; crosscut into:
    1 rectangle, 2½" × 18½"
    2 rectangles, 2½" × 10"
Cut the remaining strips into 78 various lengths
    ranging from 9½" to 16½"

From the teal print, cut:
6 strips, 2¼" × 42"

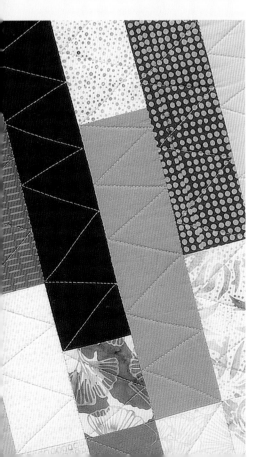

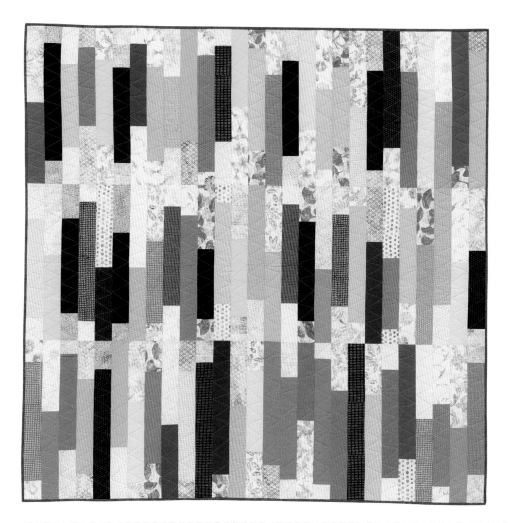

Frequency is made using one pack of Indah Pops (2½" strips) by Me + You and one Bali Poppy Waterfall (2½" strips), both from Hoffman Fabrics.

Making the Blocks

Due to the improvisational nature of this design, the exact length of each 2½"-wide piece required is not listed. The strip units may have a light rectangle sewn to both ends of a dark rectangle, or only to one end. The choice is up to you. Each strip unit should measure 2½" × 18½". Press all seam allowances open, as indicated by the arrows.

1 Sew a light 2½" × 10" rectangle to one short end of a dark rectangle to make a strip unit. Make a total of 80 units. *Do not* sew a light rectangle to the end of the dark 2½" × 18½" rectangle. Set aside the dark 2½" × 18½" rectangle for step 3.

2 For approximately 40 units, trim off 2" to 5" of the light rectangle and sew the trimmed piece to the other end of the dark rectangle to make a 3-piece unit. Trim each unit to measure 2½" × 18½". Vary the lengths of each end of the light rectangles for interest. Trim each remaining two-piece unit to measure 2½" × 18½". Make a total of 80 strip units.

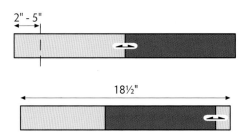

2" - 5"

18½"

3 Randomly join nine strip units along their long edges to make a block. The block should measure 18½" square, including the seam allowances. Vary the placement of the strips to create an interesting undulating design. Make eight blocks.

For the ninth block, join *eight* strip units and the dark 2½" × 18½" strip. The blocks should measure 18½" square, including the seam allowances.

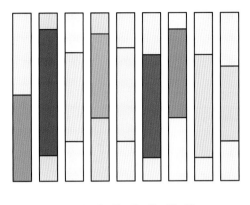

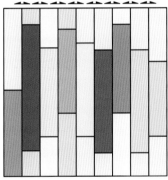

Make 9 blocks,
18½" × 18½".

SPEEDY SEWING

When joining the strip units, sew some of them together in pairs. Then join the pairs to make two four-unit sets. Join the two sets and add the last strip unit to complete the block. As you sew the pairs, alternate the sewing directions to keep the strips from warping or bending.

LEFTOVER STRIPS

Set aside the leftover strips to use in Spools on page 89. Or piece the scraps together and make extra improvisational blocks for machine-quilting practice.

Assembling the Quilt Top

1 Refer to the quilt assembly diagram below to randomly arrange the blocks in three rows of three blocks each. Sew the blocks together into rows.

2 Join the rows to complete the quilt top. The quilt top should measure 54½" square, including the seam allowances.

3 Stitch ⅛" from the edges on all four sides to prevent the edge seams from splitting open.

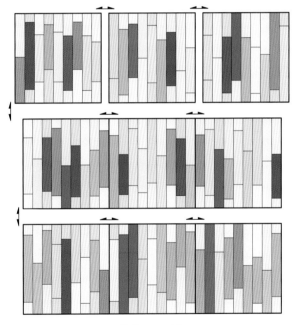

Quilt assembly

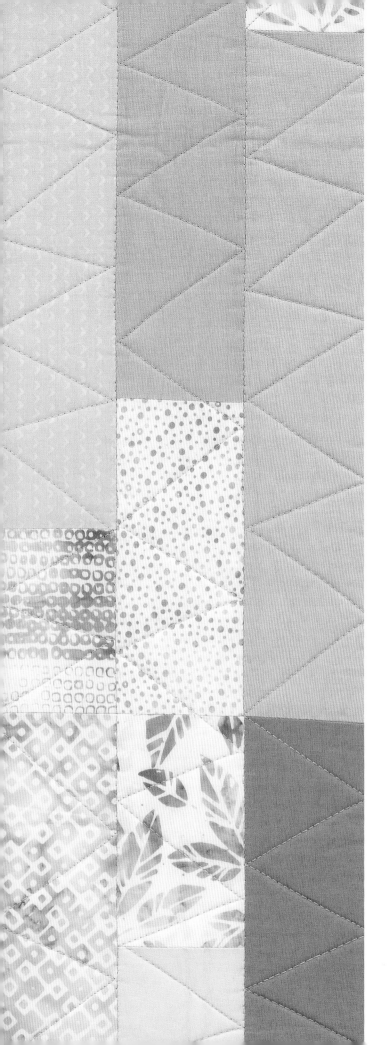

Finishing

You can find more information on piecing the backing, layering, basting, and binding your quilt at ShopMartingale.com/HowtoQuilt. Or for my particular methods, see *Machine Quilting with Style.*

1 Cut the backing yardage into two equal lengths and sew them together to make a backing approximately 6" longer and 6" wider than the quilt top.

2 Layer and baste the quilt using your favorite method.

3 Using a walking foot, quilt modern zigzags as described in "Quilting Modern Zigzags" below.

4 Trim the batting and backing flush with the quilt-top edges. Join the teal 2¼"-wide strips end to end to make one long strip. Bind the quilt edges by hand or machine using the pieced strip.

Quilting Modern Zigzags

Enjoy the beauty inherent in perfectly imperfect quilting rather than striving for computerized exactness. If possible, set your machine to stop with the needle in the down position each time you stop stitching. If your machine includes a hover feature or a knee-lift, use it to keep your hands free while pivoting the quilt. Although I quilted this design using my Bernina Dual Feed system, more experienced quilters may find it quicker and easier to free-motion quilt the design.

1 Starting in the upper right of the quilt, stitch in the ditch next to each long vertical seamline to stabilize the quilt, working your way across the quilt following lines 1–14. Start each new line of quilting 1" or 2" off the quilt in the batting (see page 11). When you reach the center, rotate the quilt 180°. Working from the center to the side, quilt anchor lines 15–26 to secure the quilt.

2 Quilt a series of random zigzag lines between two vertical seamlines, lifting the presser foot and pivoting the quilt each time you zig or zag.

3 Continue stitching zigzag lines, varying the number and spacing of the zigzags for visual appeal. The lines are short enough that you should be able to eyeball them and keep them relatively straight without marking.

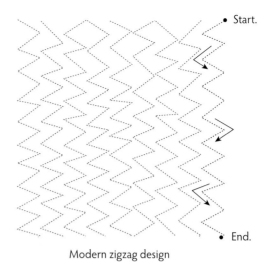

Modern zigzag design

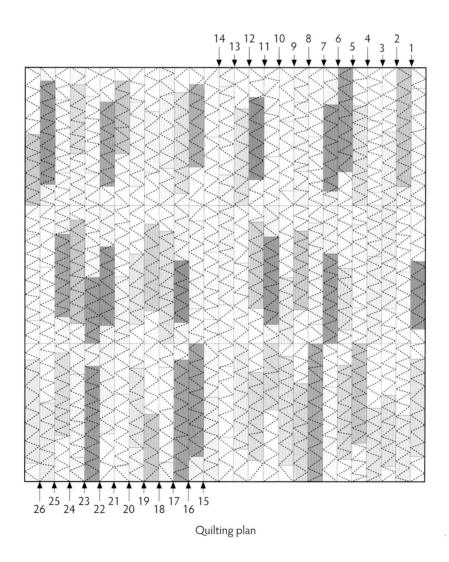

Quilting plan

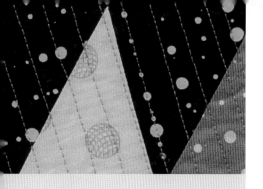

S.W.A.K.

QUILT DETAILS

- Finished quilt: 50" × 58¼"
- Finished block: 8¼" × 16½"
- Number of blocks: 15
- Batting: Hobbs Heirloom, 80% cotton/20% polyester
- Quilting thread: Aurifil 50-weight in Light Wedgewood
- Quilting designs: see "Quilting a Continuous Square Spiral" on page 40

Create a dynamic quilt to show someone you love them. Quilted with one continuous square spiral, S.W.A.K. (Sealed with a Kiss) is a great size to practice rotating the quilt.

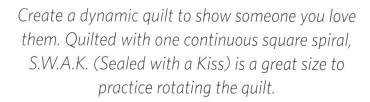

Materials

Yardage is based on 42"-wide fabric unless otherwise noted. Fat quarters measure approximately 18"×21". You can use new precut squares or leftover half-square-triangle units to make this quilt in two different sizes. (See "Use Leftover Half-Square-Triangle Units" on page 36.)

5 fat quarters (*OR* 60 squares, 5" × 5" *each*), of navy print for block background*

2 fat quarters (*OR* 24 squares, 5" × 5" *each*), of assorted light prints for block background*

7 fat quarters (*OR* 84 squares, 5" × 5" *each*), of assorted bright prints for blocks

½ yard *total* of assorted prints for scrappy binding

3¼ yards of fabric for backing

56" × 65" piece of batting

Approximately 600 yards of cotton thread for machine quilting

*For convenience in working with charm packs, you can choose all lights or all darks for the background squares, rather than the two-toned background shown in the quilt on page 37. In that case, you'll need 84 light (or dark) 5"×5" squares OR 7 fat quarters for backgrounds.

Cutting

From *each* of the navy prints, cut:

3 strips, 5" × 21"; crosscut into 12 squares,
   5" × 5" (60 total)

From *each* of the assorted light prints, cut:

3 strips, 5" × 21"; crosscut into 12 squares,
   5" × 5" (24 total)

From *each* of the assorted bright prints, cut:

3 strips, 5" × 21"; crosscut into 12 squares,
   5" × 5" (84 total)

From the assorted prints for binding, cut a *total* of:

6 strips, 2¼" × 42", or cut various lengths to
   total 230"

USE LEFTOVER HALF-SQUARE-TRIANGLE UNITS

Making S.W.A.K. using 5" squares results in a lap quilt that's 50" × 58¼". If you'd like to make a smaller wall quilt (39½" × 46"), you can start with leftover half-square-triangle units from Twinkling Diamonds on page 57. Trim the leftover units to measure 3¾" square, including the seam allowances. Follow steps 2–4 of "Making the Blocks" at right and on page 37 to make the indicated number of X and O blocks, which should each measure 7" × 13½", including the seam allowances. Make six A units (page 38) measuring 3¾" × 13½". Make 12 B units measuring 3¾" × 7". Assemble the blocks and units as instructed in "Assembling the Quilt Top" on page 39. The quilt top should be 39½" × 46".

For a scrappy binding, cut 2¼"-wide strips in various lengths to total 190". You'll need 2⅞ yards of fabric for backing and a 46" × 52" piece of batting.

Making the Blocks

Press all seam allowances open, as indicated by the arrows.

1 Mark a diagonal line from corner to corner on the wrong side of the navy and light 5" squares. With right sides together, lay a marked square on a bright square. Sew ¼" from both sides of the marked line. Cut the unit apart on the marked line to make a total of two half-square-triangle units measuring 4⅝" square, including the seam allowances. Make 120 navy units and 48 light units. Set the light units aside for "Making the Border Units" on page 38.

Make 120 units,
4⅝" × 4⅝".

Make 48 units,
4⅝" × 4⅝".

2 Sew four navy half-square-triangle units together to make a half-block unit as shown. The unit should measure 8¾" square. Make 30.

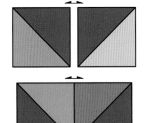 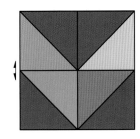

Make 30 units,
8¾" × 8¾".

S.W.A.K. is made using fat quarters of Sun Print and Abacus by Alison Glass for Andover Fabrics.

3 Lay out two half-block units, with the center triangle points touching. Join the units to make an X block measuring 8¾" × 17", including the seam allowances. Make a total of eight X blocks.

4 Lay out two half-block units, with the outer triangle points touching. Join the units to make an O block measuring 8¾" × 17", including the seam allowances. Make a total of seven O blocks.

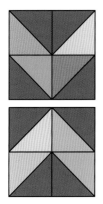
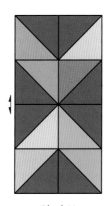

Block X.
Make 8 blocks, 8¾" × 17".

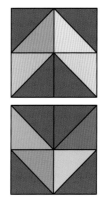
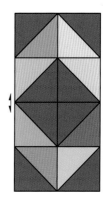

Block O.
Make 7 blocks, 8¾" × 17".

Making the Border Units

1 Join four light half-square-triangle units from step 1 of "Making the Blocks" to make an A unit. The unit should measure 4⅝" × 17". Make six A units.

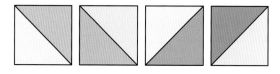

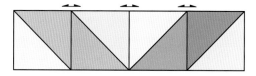

Unit A.
Make 6 units, 4⅝" × 17".

2 Join two light half-square-triangle units to make a B unit. The unit should measure 4⅝" × 8¾". Make 12 B units.

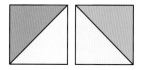

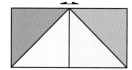

Unit B.
Make 12 units, 4⅝" × 8¾".

DIRECTIONAL PRINTS

If using fabrics with a strong directional print as I did, enjoy the interesting designs that are formed when the half-square-triangle units are sewn together randomly.

Assembling the Quilt Top

1 Refer to the quilt assembly diagram below to lay out the X and O blocks in three rows of five blocks each, alternating the blocks in each row and from row to row.

2 Place an A unit on the left and right sides of the blocks in each row, orienting the units as shown in the quilt assembly diagram to form the design.

3 Place six B units above the blocks to make the top row. Place six B units below the blocks to make the bottom row. Again, rotate the units as shown in the quilt assembly diagram.

4 Join the B units to make the top row. Repeat to make the bottom row. Join the A units and blocks in each row. Then sew the rows together to complete the quilt top. The quilt top should measure 50" × 58¼", including the seam allowances.

5 Stitch ⅛" from the edges on all four sides to prevent the edge seams from splitting open.

Finishing

You can find more information on piecing the backing, layering, basting, and binding your quilt at ShopMartingale.com/HowtoQuilt. Or for my particular methods, see *Machine Quilting with Style*.

1 Cut the backing yardage into two equal lengths and sew them together to make a backing approximately 6" longer and 6" wider than the quilt top.

2 Layer and baste the quilt using your favorite method.

3 Using a walking foot, quilt a continuous square spiral as described in "Quilting a Continuous Square Spiral" on page 40.

4 Trim the batting and backing flush with the quilt-top edges. Join the print 2¼"-wide strips end to end to make one long strip. Bind the quilt edges by hand or machine using the pieced strip.

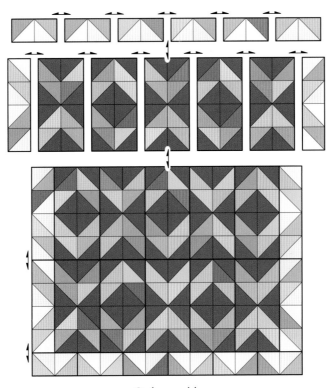

Quilt assembly

Quilting a Continuous Square Spiral

The idea for this quilting motif came from merging two designs in my first book. Combining a square spiral with a continuous circle technique creates an interesting straight-line design that doesn't need to be marked! How fun would it be to quilt continuous spirals starting with different center shapes like triangles, diamonds, or hexagons?

The trick is to keep your lines straight and even around the turn by counting the number of stitches to make each time you pivot. First, measure the width of the line spacing you'll use (the width from your needle to the edge of your presser foot). Next, count how many stitches will fit into that measurement. For example, my line spacing is ½", and it takes my machine five stitches to travel that distance. Sew this many stitches beyond your turning point each time you rotate the quilt. You may want to practice the center spiral on a scrap first to get the spacing right.

Stitch the same number of stitches past the previous line each time you pivot the quilt.

1 Starting in the center of your quilt, bring the bobbin thread to the top (see page 12) and quilt the number of stitches equal to the width of your line spacing. Stitch the first line (approximately 5 stitches) and stop with your needle down in the fabric. Lift the presser foot, and rotate the quilt 90° clockwise to stitch the next line.

2 Continue quilting and rotating clockwise with the same number of stitches per side until you have stitched a small center square. When you reach the starting point, continue quilting the same number of stitches past the starting point and pivot to continue the spiral in a clockwise direction. Once you have started echoing around the center square, use the edge of the presser foot as a guide right next to

the previous line of stitching for consistent spacing. Remember to count stitches each time your needle is parallel to the corner of the previously stitched line.

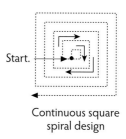

Start.

Continuous square
spiral design

3 Continue quilting in a clockwise direction to fill the entire space, pivoting the quilt at the corners to continue the spiral. Once you've stitched four to five spirals, the quilting becomes easier because you can quilt longer lines before turning the quilt. If your lines start to get a bit wonky relative to the seamlines, slightly veer them back on track and use the seamlines as a guide to keep your lines straight.

4 Quilt off the edge of the quilt when you run out of space to quilt. Add additional straight lines of quilting to the top and bottom edges, lining up the edge of your presser foot with the previous line of stitching for correct line spacing.

Quilting plan

Free-Motion Quilting

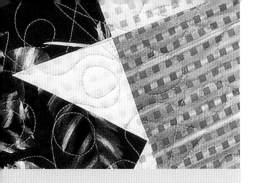

STARSTRUCK

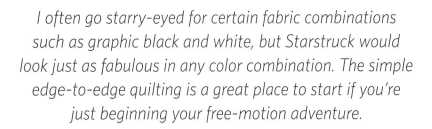

QUILT DETAILS

- Finished quilt: 54½" × 78½"
- Finished blocks: 12" × 12"
- Number of blocks: 24
- Batting: Quilters Dream Cotton, Request Loft
- Quilting thread: Aurifil 50-weight in Sand
- Quilting designs: see "Quilting Loops and Stars" on page 48

I often go starry-eyed for certain fabric combinations such as graphic black and white, but Starstruck would look just as fabulous in any color combination. The simple edge-to-edge quilting is a great place to start if you're just beginning your free-motion adventure.

Materials

Yardage is based on 42"-wide fabric. Fat quarters measure approximately 18" × 21".

12 fat quarters of dark gray to black prints (referred to collectively as "dark") for blocks and border

12 fat quarters of light gray, tan, and white prints (referred to collectively as "light") for blocks and border

½ yard of black solid for binding

4¾ yards of fabric for backing

61" × 85" piece of batting

Approximately 1,200 yards of cotton thread for machine quilting

Cutting

Refer to the fat quarter cutting diagram below as you cut the fat quarters. Each fat quarter will yield 1 Star block and 4 border squares. Label all pieces for easy reference. For quicker cutting, layer up to four fat quarters. If you're working with directional prints, don't worry if the prints go in different directions—that will add variety.

From *each* fat quarter, cut:

1 strip, 7" × 21"; crosscut into:
    1 square, 7" × 7"; cut the square into 4 A squares,
        3½" × 3½" (96 total; 12 are extra)
    1 B square, 6¼" × 6¼" (24 total)
    1 C square, 5½" × 5½" (24 total)
1 strip, 3⅜" × 21"; crosscut into:
    4 D squares, 3⅜" × 3⅜" (96 total)
    2 E squares, 3" × 3" (48 total)
1 strip, 3" × 21"; crosscut into:
    2 E squares, 3" × 3" (48 total)
    1 F rectangle, 2½" × 10½" (24 total)
1 G rectangle, 2½" × 12½" (24 total)

From the black solid, cut:

7 strips, 2¼" × 42"

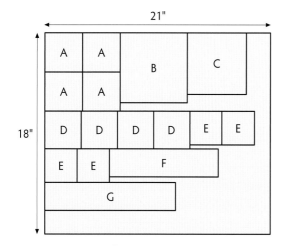

Fat quarter cutting

Making the Blocks

Press all seam allowances open, as indicated by the arrows.

1 Place two dark D squares on opposite corners of one light B square as shown, right sides together. The smaller squares will overlap slightly. Draw a diagonal line from corner to corner across the D squares. Pin the squares in place to keep them from shifting. Sew ¼" from both sides of the marked line. Cut the unit apart on the marked line and press.

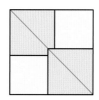 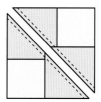

2 Place one of the remaining dark D squares on the large triangle corner of one unit from step 1, right sides together. Mark a diagonal line on the dark D square as shown. Stitch ¼" from both sides of the marked line, and then cut the unit apart on the marked line to make two flying-geese units. Press and trim the dog-eared triangle tips. Repeat with the remaining unit from step 1 to make a total of four star-point units measuring 3" × 5½" each.

Make 4 units,
3" × 5½".

Starstruck is made using 24 assorted fat quarters by Jennifer Sampou from Robert Kaufman Fabrics.

3 Using the same fabrics as in step 1, lay out one dark C square, the star-point units from step 2, and four light E squares as shown. Sew the squares and units together in rows. Join the rows to make a star unit. Sew a light F rectangle to the bottom of the star unit. Sew a light G rectangle to the right side of the unit to complete the block. The block should measure 12½" square, including the seam allowances. Make a total of 12 blocks with dark stars and light backgrounds.

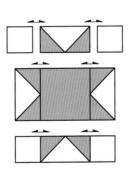

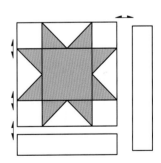

Make 12 blocks, 12½" × 12½".

4 Reversing the fabric colors, repeat steps 1–3 to make 12 blocks with light stars and dark backgrounds. The blocks should measure 12½" square, including the seam allowances.

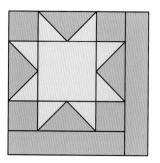

Make 12 blocks,
12½" × 12½".

PERFECT POINTS

When joining triangle units, pin generously and sew through the X intersection on the wrong side of the unit. It's OK if you need to sew a scant ¼" seam allowance. A floating point will look much better than a chopped-off one.

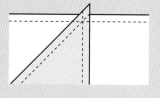

Assembling the Quilt Top

1 Refer to the quilt assembly diagram to lay out the blocks in six rows of four blocks each, rotating the blocks in each row and from row to row as desired to create a pleasing arrangement. Notice that the dark Star blocks are located in the upper two rows and the left half of the middle two rows. The light Star blocks are located in the right half of the middle two rows and all of the lower two rows.

2 Sew the blocks together into rows. Join the rows to complete the quilt center. Press. The quilt center should measure 48½" × 72½", including the seam allowances.

3 Join 12 light and 12 dark A squares, alternating them as shown, to make a side border measuring 3½" × 72½". Make two side border strips. Press all seam allowances open.

Side borders.
Make 2 borders, 3½" × 72½".

4 To make the top border, join 9 light and 9 dark A squares, alternating them as shown. Press all seam allowances open. The border should measure 3½" × 54½". Repeat to make the bottom border.

Top/Bottom borders.
Make 2 borders, 3½" × 54½".

5 Rotating the borders as needed so that the light/ dark pattern is continuous around the quilt, sew the side borders to opposite sides of the quilt center. Add the top and bottom borders to complete the quilt top. The quilt top should measure 54½" × 78½", including the seam allowances.

6 Stitch ⅛" from the edges on all four sides to prevent the edge seams from splitting open.

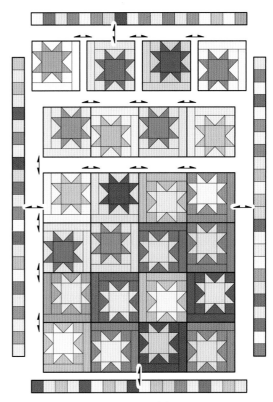

Quilt assembly

Finishing

You can find more information on piecing the backing, layering, basting, and binding your quilt at ShopMartingale.com/HowtoQuilt. Or for my particular methods, see *Machine Quilting with Style*.

1 Cut the backing yardage into two equal lengths and join them to make a backing approximately 6" longer and 6" wider than the quilt top.

2 Layer and baste the quilt using your favorite method.

3 Drop the feed dogs and use a free-motion foot to quilt loops and stars as described in "Quilting Loops and Stars" on page 48.

4 Trim the batting and backing flush with the quilt-top edges. Join the black 2¼"-wide strips end to end to make one long strip. Bind the quilt edges by hand or machine using the pieced strip.

Quilting Loops and Stars

An allover design, also known as "edge-to-edge" quilting, is one of the easiest and quickest ways to jump into free-motion quilting. The motif is quilted independently of the block design, allowing you to blur the seamlines and hide any piecing irregularities. It's the perfect choice to use on a quilt top that won't quite lie flat. You can move around the quilt, easing in any fullness as needed. Just be sure to choose a neutral thread color that blends well with the majority of the fabrics in the quilt.

1 Before starting, take a few minutes to sketch the loops and stars design on a piece of paper. This will help your hands warm up and will train your brain to form the design. Try combining loops with other fun designs such as hearts, flowers, leaves, or anything else you can think of!

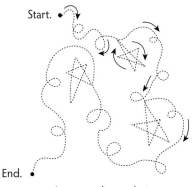

Loops and stars design

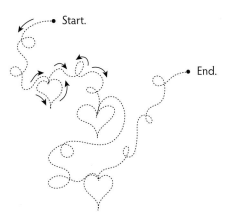

Loops and hearts design

2 Start stitching anywhere near the edge of the quilt top in the excess batting. Stitch a few inches to catch your threads and ensure that your tension is set properly. Then move the quilt so that the needle stitches into the quilt top, being careful not to catch the edge of the top in the presser foot.

3 Gently make a smooth curving line and then form a loop. Stitch another gently curving line and then briefly pause before beginning the star. Stitch straight down for an inch or two, trying to maintain a nice, straight line. Move up and to the right, over to the left, diagonally down to the right, and then back up again, closing the star at its starting point. Pause for a brief second to catch your breath, and then quilt another loop on the opposite side of the star.

4 Quilt a gently curving line again and then go into another loop-and-star combination. Get comfortable quilting the motif in different directions as you make your way around the quilt. For variety, change the direction of the loops or the number of loops between the stars.

5 Continue with the motif combination to cover the entire quilt area, stitching your way around the quilt in rows or quadrants. Don't be afraid to rotate the quilt as needed to get a better position. Try quilting an entire block section before moving on to the next section. Quilt off the edge every now and then to check your bobbin.

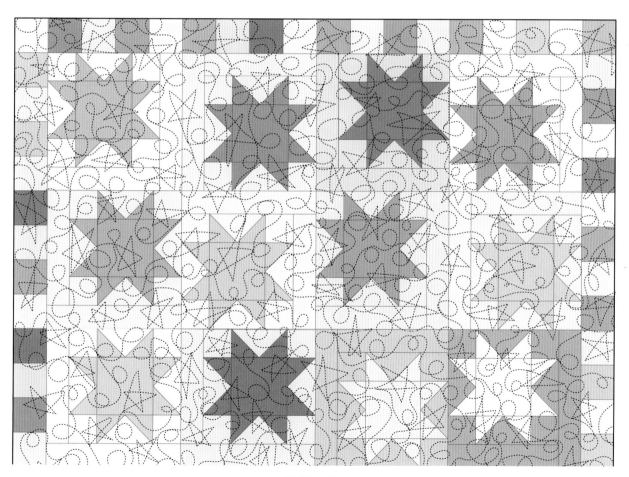

Quilting plan

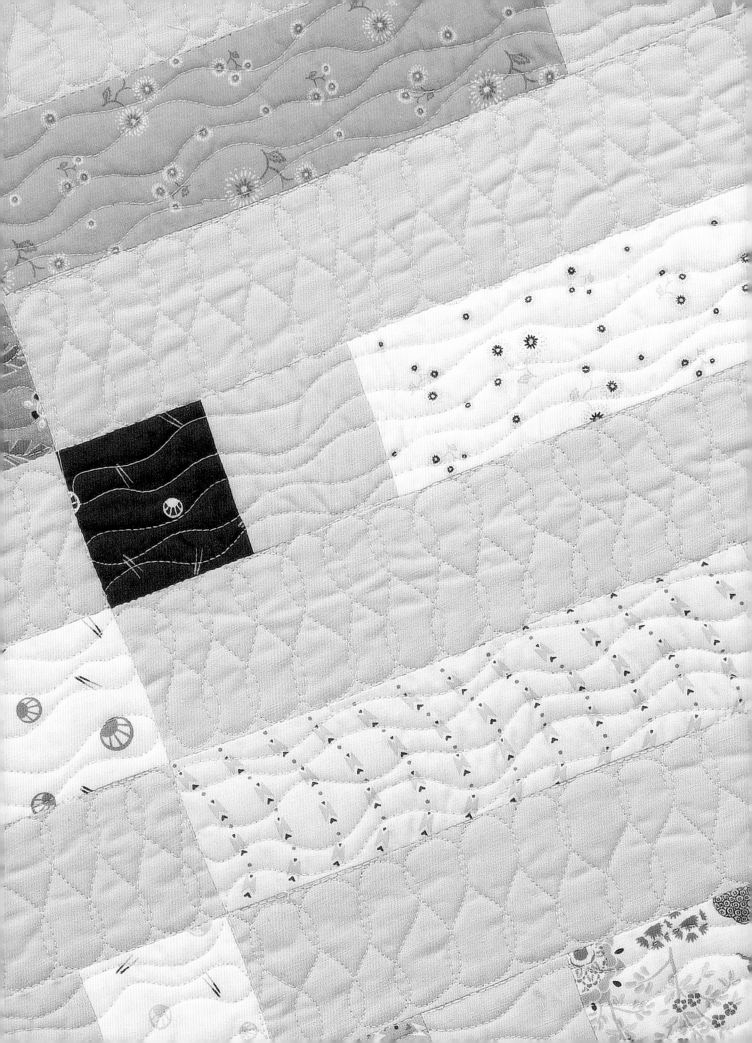

DOT 'N' DASH

QUILT DETAILS

- Finished quilt: 60½" × 72½"
- Finished blocks: 12" × 12"
- Number of blocks: 30
- Batting: Hobbs Tuscany Wool
- Quilting thread: Aurifil 50-weight in Light Grey Blue
- Quilting designs: see "Quilting Wavy Lines and Crazy Eights" on page 55

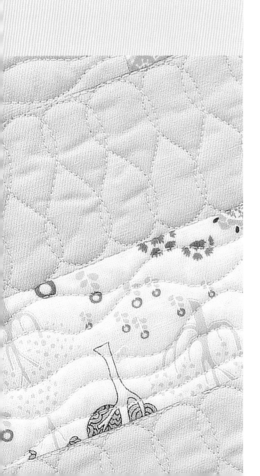

Combine your favorite print and solid strips into a graphic, modern quilt that's the perfect place to practice continuous custom quilting.

Materials

Yardage is based on 42"-wide fabric.

40 strips, 2½" × 42" *each*, of assorted prints for blocks and binding

36 strips, 2½" × 42" *each*, of gray solid for background

4 yards of fabric for backing

67" × 79" piece of batting

Approximately 1,200 yards of cotton thread for machine quilting

Cutting

From *each of 30* assorted strips, cut:*
2 rectangles, 2½" × 8½" (60 total)
2 squares, 2½" × 2½" (60 total)

From *each of 10* assorted strips, cut:
3 rectangles, 2½" × 8½" (30 total)
3 squares, 2½" × 2½" (30 total)

From *each of 30* gray strips, cut:
3 rectangles, 2½" × 12½" (90 total)

From the 6 remaining gray strips, cut a *total* of:
90 squares, 2½" × 2½"

*Set aside the remaining strips for a scrappy binding.

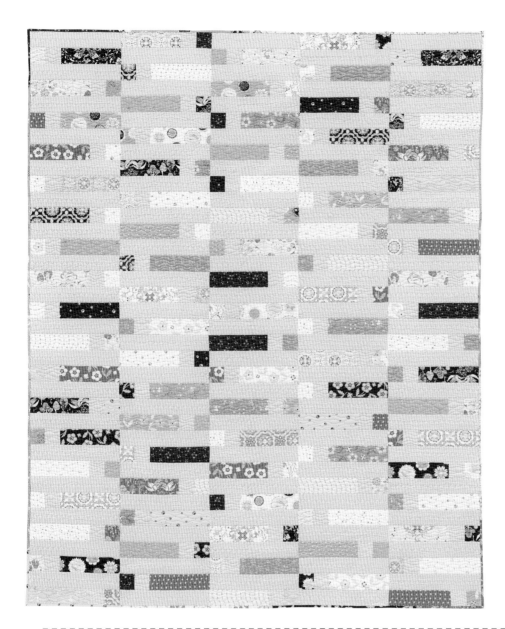

Dot 'n' Dash is made using one Manderley Jelly Roll (2½" strips) by Franny and Jane and two Bella Solids Zen Gray Junior Jelly Rolls (2½" strips), both from Moda Fabrics.

Making the Blocks

Press all seam allowances open, as indicated by the arrows.

1 Join a print and a gray 2½" square to make a two-patch unit. Sew a different print 2½" × 8½" rectangle to the gray square to make a three-patch unit. The unit should measure 2½" × 12½". Make 90.

Make 90 units, 2½" × 12½".

2 Starting with a gray strip, lay out three different units from step 1 and three gray 2½" × 12½" rectangles, placing two print squares on the left side of the block and one print square on the right side. Sew the pieces together along their long edges to make an A block measuring 12½" square, including the seam allowances. Make 15 A blocks.

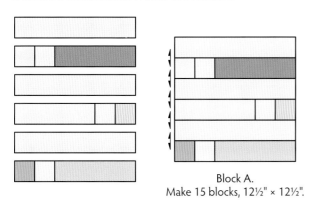

Block A.
Make 15 blocks, 12½" × 12½".

3 Starting with a gray strip, lay out three different units from step 1 and three gray 2½" × 12½" rectangles, placing two print squares on the right side of the block and one print square on the left side. Sew the pieces together along their long edges to make a B block measuring 12½" square, including the seam allowances. Make 15 B blocks.

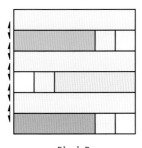

Block B.
Make 15 blocks, 12½" × 12½".

OPPOSING DIRECTIONS

To prevent the blocks from warping, keep the gray strips on top while joining the strips and units. That way you'll automatically reverse directions as you sew.

LEFTOVER STRIPS

Trim some of the leftover strips to 2¼" wide and use them as a scrappy binding on another project. Or use the strips to make blocks for machine-quilting practice.

Assembling the Quilt Top

1 Sew together five A blocks with the strips oriented horizontally. Rotate every other block so that the second and fourth blocks in the row have the gray strip on the bottom of the block. The row should measure 12½" × 60½", including the seam allowances. Repeat to make a total of three A rows.

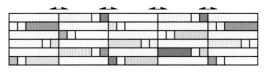

Row A.
Make 3 rows, 12½" × 60½".

2 Sew together five B blocks with the strips oriented horizontally. Rotate every other block so that the second and fourth blocks in the row have the gray strip on the bottom of the block. The row should measure 12½" × 60½", including the seam allowances. Repeat to make a total of three B rows.

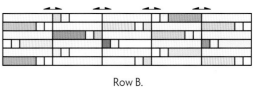

Row B.
Make 3 rows, 12½" × 60½".

3 Refer to the quilt assembly diagram on page 54 to lay out the A and B rows, alternating them to form the design. Join the rows to complete the quilt top, which should measure 60½" × 72½", including the seam allowances.

4 Stitch ⅛" from the edges on all four sides to prevent the edge seams from splitting open.

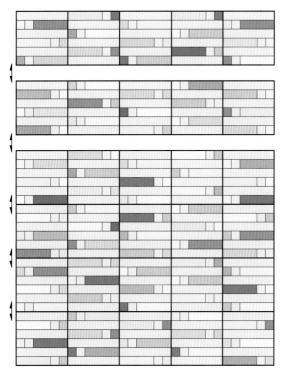

Quilt assembly

Finishing

You can find more information on piecing the backing, layering, basting, and binding your quilt at ShopMartingale.com/HowtoQuilt. Or for my particular methods, see *Machine Quilting with Style*.

1 Cut the backing yardage into two equal pieces and join them to make a backing approximately 6" longer and 6" wider than the quilt top.

2 Layer and baste the quilt using your favorite method.

3 If desired, use a walking foot to stitch in the ditch between all of the horizontal rows to anchor the quilt. Then, drop the feed dogs and use a free-motion foot to quilt wavy lines and crazy eights as described in "Quilting Wavy Lines and Crazy Eights," opposite.

4 Trim the batting and backing flush with the quilt-top edges. Join the remaining print 2½"-wide strips end to end to make a 280"-long strip. (If desired, trim the strips to 2¼" wide.) Bind the quilt edges by hand or machine using the pieced strip.

BETTER BINDING

When working with a scrappy binding you'll have a lot of seams, which means a higher likelihood that a seam will end up in a corner. To prevent this, pin the starting end of your binding anywhere on the quilt. Quickly measure the binding around the perimeter of the quilt to see if any of the seams will fall in the corners. If they do, adjust the starting position of the binding until no seam lands in a corner, and then sew the binding on as you normally would.

Quilting Wavy Lines and Crazy Eights

Wavy lines are basically the free-motion version of squiggles quilting shown on page 19. Free-motion quilting allows you to quilt multiple wavy lines back and forth, without stopping to pivot. The crazy eights motif is a faster version of ribbon candy shown on page 70. When quilting these motifs, rotate the quilt as needed to get in a comfortable position. I can quilt the wavy lines in either direction, but it feels more natural to quilt the crazy eights from side to side, going from right to left. While quilting crazy eights, it was necessary for me to rotate the quilt each time I reached the midpoint of a row so the quilt would fit in the machine and I could continue quilting continuously.

1 To quilt wavy lines, begin in the corner of a three-patch unit. Quilt a series of wavy lines back and forth, parallel to the long edge. Add a curve to the end of each line as you switch direction and quilt another wavy line in the opposite direction. Quilt an odd number of lines so that you finish quilting the unit on the end that's opposite where you started. Stitch in the ditch between the rectangles to get to the next unit to be quilted. Quilt all of the three-patch units the same way, covering two rows in one pass **(fig. 1)**.

2 To quilt crazy eights, begin in the top corner of a gray rectangle and quilt an *S* shape. When you reach the bottom of the *S*, quilt back up, forming a backward *S*, overlapping your previous line. Quilt a series of crazy eights motifs to fill in the space. Quilt all of the gray rectangles the same way, covering two rows in one pass **(fig. 2)**.

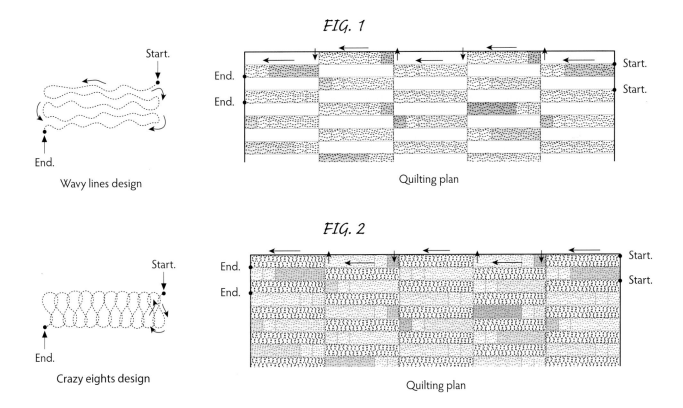

FIG. 1

Start.

End.

Wavy lines design

End.
End.

Start.
Start.

Quilting plan

FIG. 2

Start.

End.

Crazy eights design

End.
End.

Start.
Start.

Quilting plan

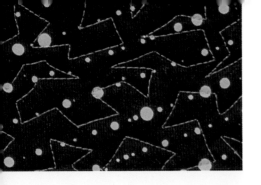

TWINKLING DIAMONDS

QUILT DETAILS

- Finished quilt: 76½" × 88½"
- Finished block: 8" × 12"
- Number of blocks: 31
- Batting: Quilters Dream Wool
- Quilting thread: Aurifil 50-weight in Light Wedgewood and Light Grey Blue
- Quilting designs: see "Quilting Jagged Stipple, Wavy Lines, and Cursive Ls" on page 62

Let your quilting skills sparkle in the diamond blocks of this colorful design. As an added bonus, you'll have enough leftover pieces to make a smaller companion piece.

Materials

Yardage is based on 42"-wide fabric. Fat quarters measure approximately 18" × 21" and fat eighths measure 9" × 21".

6½ yards of navy print for background, borders, and binding

16 fat quarters of assorted bright prints for blocks

16 fat eighths of assorted light prints for block centers

7⅜ yards of fabric for backing

85" × 97" piece of batting

Approximately 1,800 yards of cotton thread for machine quilting the background

Approximately 600 yards of cotton thread for machine quilting the diamonds

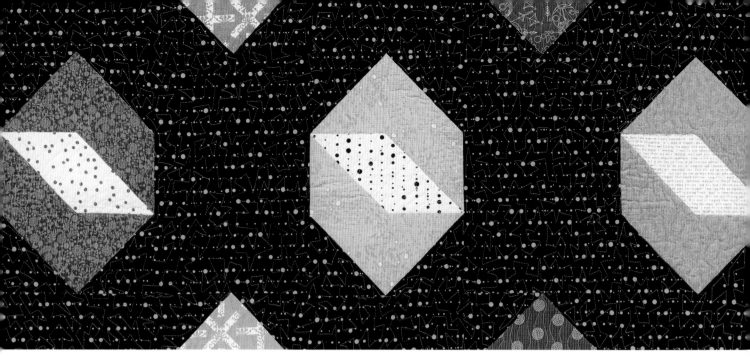

Cutting

From the *crosswise* grain of the navy print, cut:
11 strips, 8½" × 42"; crosscut into 32 rectangles,
    8½" × 12½"
5 strips, 2½" × 42"
9 strips, 2¼" × 42"

From the *lengthwise* grain of the navy print, cut:*
2 strips, 2½" × 76½"

**From the *crosswise* grain of the remaining navy
print, cut:**
18 strips, 4½" × 35"; crosscut into 124 squares,
    4½" × 4½"

From *each* assorted bright print, cut:
3 strips, 4½" × 21"; crosscut into:
    4 rectangles, 4½" × 8½" (64 total; 2 are extra)
    4 squares, 4½" × 4½" (64 total; 2 are extra)

From *each* assorted light print, cut:
1 strip, 4½" × 21"; crosscut into 2 rectangles,
    4½" × 8½" (32 total; 1 is extra)

**If using a nondirectional print, cut 4 strips, 2½" × 42",
and 16 strips, 4½" × 42", from the crosswise grain
instead of the lengthwise grain.*

Making the Blocks

Press all seam allowances open, as indicated by
the arrows.

1 Mark a diagonal line from corner to corner on
the wrong side of each navy 4½" square. Mark
a second diagonal line ½" from the first line. Place a
marked square on the left end of a bright 4½" × 8½"
rectangle, right sides together and raw edges aligned.
Be sure to orient the square as shown, with the
shorter marked line above the longer line. Stitch on
both marked lines and cut between the two lines.
Flip the resulting triangle open and press. Make 62.

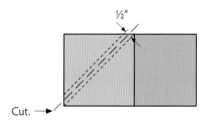

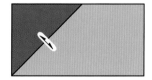

Make 62 units,
4½" × 8½".

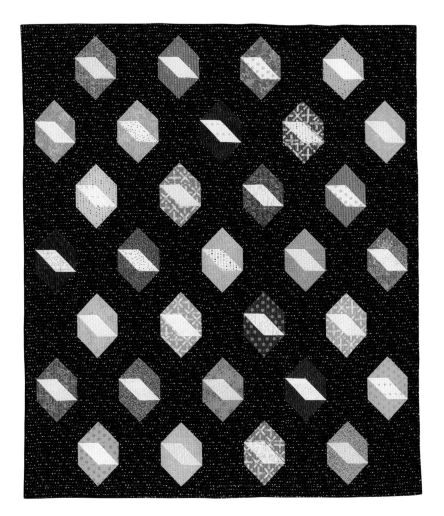

Twinkling Diamonds is made using 16 fat quarters of Sun Print and 16 fat eighths of Abacus by Alison Glass from Andover Fabrics.

USING DIRECTIONAL PRINTS

To ensure that a directional print is oriented the same way throughout the quilt, separate the squares into two piles of 62 squares each, with the print running the same direction in both piles. Mark the diagonal lines so that the lines are going in opposite directions for each pile.

Mark 32 of each.

2 Place a second marked navy square on the right end of the unit from step 1, right sides together and raw edges aligned. Be sure to orient the square as before, with the shorter marked line above the longer line. Stitch on both marked lines and cut between the two lines to make a flying-geese unit measuring 4½" × 8½". Make 62 units.

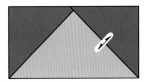

Make 62 units, 4½" × 8½".

3 Mark a diagonal line from corner to corner on the wrong side of each bright 4½" square. Mark a second diagonal line ½" from the first line. Repeating step 1, stitch, cut, and press a marked bright square on the left end of a light 4½" × 8½" rectangle. In the same way, stitch, cut, and press a marked bright square on the right end of the light rectangle, making sure that both squares are oriented with the marked lines in the same direction as shown. The unit should measure 4½" × 8½", including the seam allowances. Make 31 center units. See "Bonus Units" below to use the cut-away triangles.

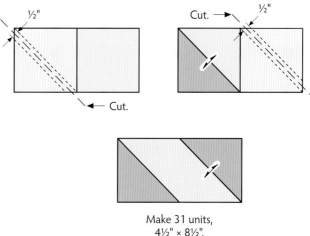

Make 31 units,
4½" × 8½".

BONUS UNITS

Here are a couple ideas for using the bonus half-square-triangle units from step 3. Press the seam allowances open on all the units. The units should measure 3¾" square, including the seam allowances. It's OK if your measurements are different; simply trim them all to the same size. You can use 120 navy/bright and 48 light/bright units to make S.W.A.K. on page 35, although the result will be a smaller quilt, 39½" × 46". Or use the additional leftover units to make blocks for machine-quilting practice.

4 Lay out two flying-geese units and one center unit, making sure the bright print is the same in all three units. Join the units to make a block measuring 8½" × 12½", including the seam allowances. Make a total of 31 blocks.

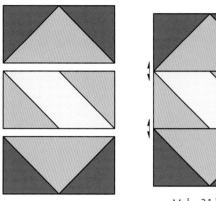

Make 31 blocks,
8½" × 12½".

Assembling the Quilt Top

1 Refer to the quilt assembly diagram to lay out the blocks and navy 8½" × 12½" rectangles in seven rows, alternating them in each row and from row to row as shown. Sew the blocks and rectangles together into rows. Join the rows to complete the quilt-top center. The quilt-top center should measure 72½" × 84½", including the seam allowances.

2 Join the navy 2½" × 42" strips end to end. From the long strip, cut two 84½"-long strips. Sew the strips to opposite sides of the quilt top. The quilt top should measure 76½" × 84½", including the seam allowances.

3 Sew the navy 2½" × 76½" strips to the top and bottom of the quilt top. The quilt top should measure 76½" × 88½", including the seam allowances.

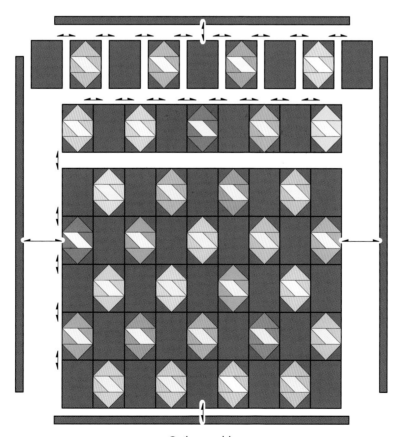

Quilt assembly

Finishing

You can find more information on piecing the backing, layering, basting, and binding your quilt at ShopMartingale.com/HowtoQuilt. Or for my particular methods, see *Machine Quilting with Style*.

1 Cut the backing yardage into three equal pieces and sew them together to make a backing approximately 8" longer and 8" wider than the quilt top.

2 Layer and baste the quilt using your favorite method.

3 Drop the feed dogs and use a free-motion foot to quilt jagged stipple in the background. Then quilt wavy lines and cursive *L*s in the blocks as described in "Quilting Jagged Stipple, Wavy Lines, and Cursive *L*s," below.

4 Trim the batting and backing flush with the quilt-top edges. Join the navy 2¼"-wide strips end to end to make one long strip. Bind the quilt edges by hand or machine using the pieced strip.

Quilting Jagged Stipple, Wavy Lines, and Cursive Ls

If you use the same-colored thread in the background and blocks, you can quilt the entire quilt from edge to edge, while still providing a custom-quilted look. The key is to use a lightweight thread that will look good on both light and dark fabrics. My fabrics have such a high contrast that I chose to quilt the background with a darker blue thread, and the blocks with a light blue thread, starting and stopping between blocks.

1 Quilt jagged stipple in all of the background areas, working your way around the quilt. When you get to a Diamond block, slowly stitch in the ditch around the outside of the block to anchor it as you free motion quilt. If using two different thread colors, quilt all of the background before moving on to the blocks.

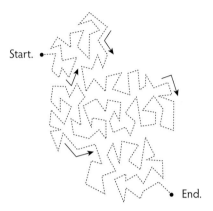

Jagged stipple design

2 To quilt the Diamond block, stitch in the ditch around the inner diamond (lines 1–4). Then fill the center with cursive *L*s (line 5). Last, fill in the diamond shape with a series of wavy lines about ¼" to ½" apart, backtracking in the seamlines to get to the next line (lines 6–7).

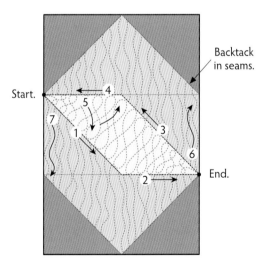

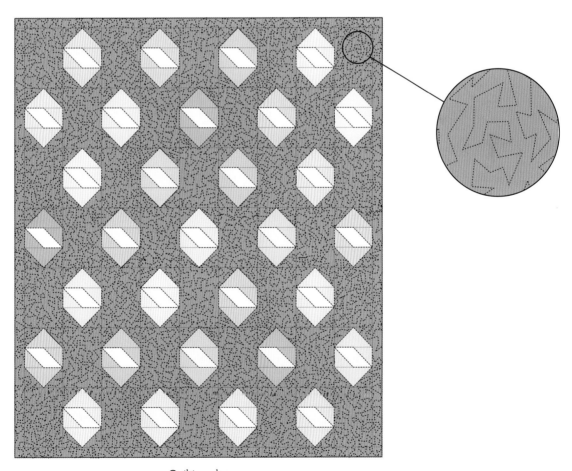

Quilting plan

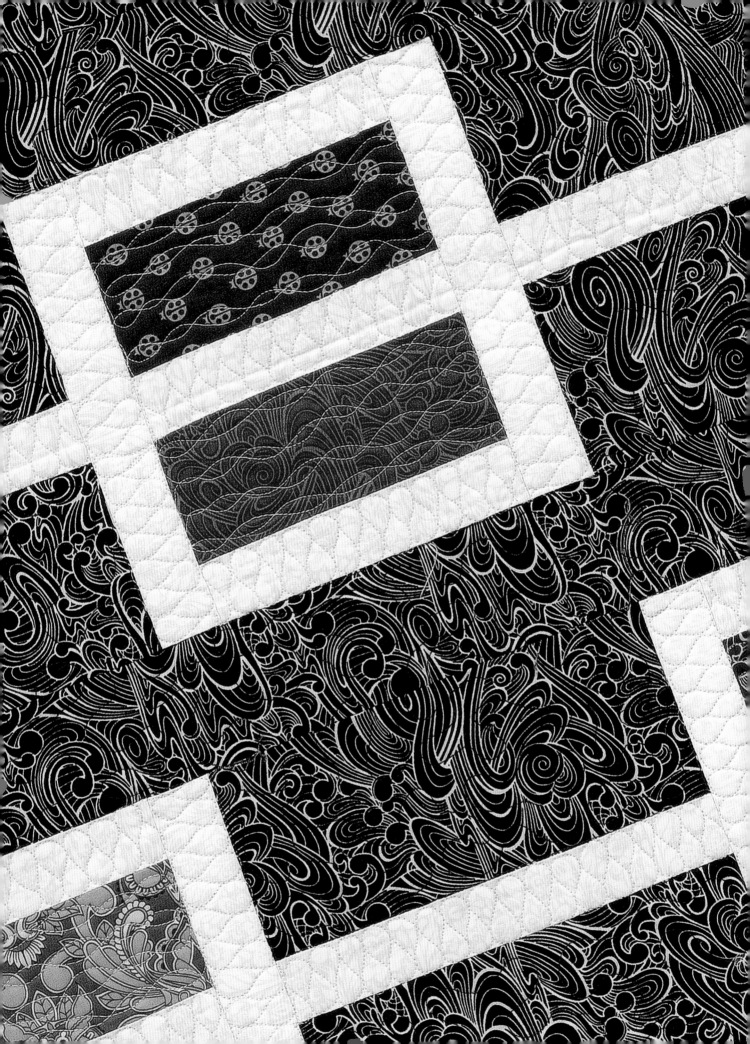

WINDOWS

QUILT DETAILS

- Finished quilt: 67½" × 83½"
- Finished block: 7" × 7"
- Number of blocks: 71
- Batting: Warm and Natural Cotton
- Quilting thread: Aurifil 50-weight in Very Dark Gray and Shell
- Quilting designs: see "Quilting Stipples, Ribbon Candy, and Free-Form Cables" on page 69

Although this quilt is made up of mostly negative space that can be quilted quickly, the pattern is perfect for showcasing a smaller group of precut strips from your favorite fabric designer.

Materials

Yardage is based on 42"-wide fabric unless otherwise noted.

1⅞ yards of light gray print for blocks

12 strips, 2½" × 42", of assorted prints for blocks

4⅛ yards of black print for background, sashing, and binding

5¼ yards of fabric for backing

76" × 92" piece of batting

Approximately 1,200 yards of cotton thread for machine quilting the background

Approximately 1,200 yards of cotton thread for machine quilting the blocks

FABRIC SELECTION

Choose a busy, nondirectional background print to hide the seams, so the blocks appear to float. For a scrappy look, choose a variety of background prints from the same color family. For more variety in the blocks, use 24 strips that are 21" long.

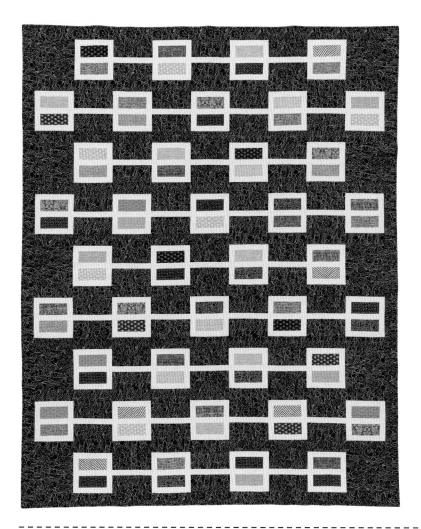

Windows is made using one Tula Pink Design Roll (2½" strips) from Free Spirit Fabrics.

Cutting

From the light gray print, cut:

40 strips, 1½" × 42"; crosscut into:
    111 rectangles, 1½" × 7½"
    120 rectangles, 1½" × 5½"

From *each* of the assorted print strips, cut:

7 rectangles, 2½" × 5½" (84 total; 4 are extra)

From the black print, cut:

13 strips, 3½" × 42"; crosscut into 62 rectangles,
    3½" × 7½"
2 strips, 7½" × 42"; crosscut into 10 squares,
    7½" × 7½"
29 strips, 2½" × 42"

QUICK CUTTING AND COUNTING

Stack two folded strips atop one another, so you're cutting four layers of fabric at a time. That way you can count by multiples of four. For example, if you need 120 rectangles, you'd have 30 stacks of four rectangles each. Stack each set of four rectangles, crisscrossing them to make counting easier.

When cutting yardage into strips, speed up the process by folding the fabric in half lengthwise and then widthwise so you're cutting through four layers. Then you'll cut two strips at a time instead of just one.

Making Block A

Press all seam allowances open, as indicated by the arrows.

1 Join a gray 1½" × 5½" rectangle and a print 2½" × 5½" rectangle to make a 3½" × 5½" unit. Make a total of 80 units.

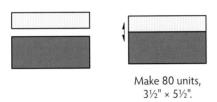

Make 80 units,
3½" × 5½".

2 Join a gray 1½" × 5½" rectangle and two different units from step 1 as shown. The unit should measure 5½" × 7½". Make a total of 40 units.

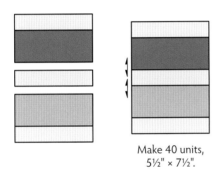

Make 40 units,
5½" × 7½".

3 Sew gray 1½" × 7½" rectangles to opposite sides of a unit from step 2 to make block A. The block should measure 7½" square, including the seam allowances. Make a total of 40 A blocks.

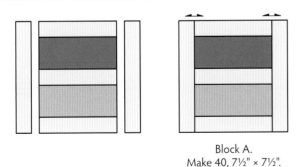

Block A.
Make 40, 7½" × 7½".

Making Block B

Sew black 3½" × 7½" rectangles to both long sides of a gray 1½" × 7½" rectangle to make block B. Press. The block should measure 7½" square, including the seam allowances. Make a total of 31 B blocks.

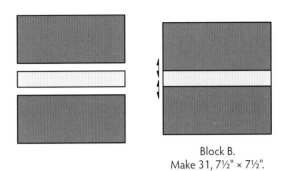

Block B.
Make 31, 7½" × 7½".

Assembling the Quilt Top

1 Join four A blocks, three B blocks, and two black squares to make a row. The row should measure 7½" × 63½", including the seam allowances. Make a total of five A rows.

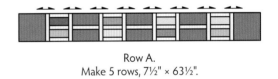

Row A.
Make 5 rows, 7½" × 63½".

2 Sew five A blocks and four B blocks together to make a row. The row should measure 7½" × 63½", including the seam allowances. Make a total of four B rows.

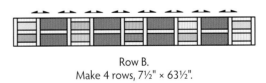

Row B.
Make 4 rows, 7½" × 63½".

3 Join 21 of the black 2½" × 42" strips end to end. From the pieced strip, cut 10 strips, 2½" × 63½", for the top and bottom borders and the horizontal sashing. Cut two 2½" × 83½" strips for the side borders.

MEASURE TWICE, CUT ONCE!

If your seams tend to grow or shrink, measure the length of the block rows and cut 10 horizontal strips to that exact measurement. Join the block rows, horizontal sashing, and top and bottom borders. Then measure the length of the quilt top; cut two vertical strips to that exact measurement for the side borders.

To make measuring easier, fold the strip in half and place it on a long mat. Measure half the distance needed, starting from the folded end. For example, if you need a 63½"-long strip, measure 31¾" from the fold and trim the strip. Just be sure you cut from the open end, not the folded end.

4 Refer to the quilt assembly diagram below to lay out the A and B rows and the black 63½"-long strips, alternating them as shown. Sew the rows and strips together. Press the seam allowances open. The quilt top should measure 63½" × 83½", including the seam allowances.

5 Sew the black 83½"-long strips to opposite sides of the quilt top. The quilt top should now measure 67½" × 83½", including the seam allowances.

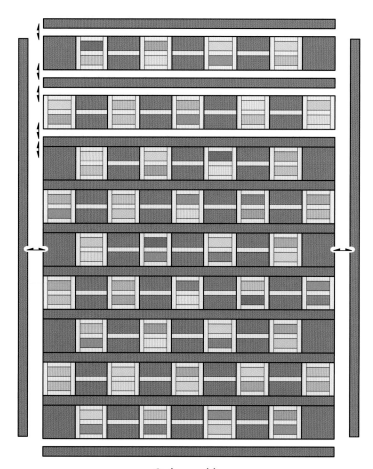

Quilt assembly

Finishing

You can find more information on piecing the backing, layering, basting, and binding your quilt at ShopMartingale.com/HowtoQuilt. Or for my particular methods, see *Machine Quilting with Style*.

1 Cut the backing yardage into two equal pieces and sew them together to make a backing approximately 8" longer and 8" wider than the quilt top.

2 Layer and baste the quilt using your favorite method.

3 Drop the feed dogs and use a free-motion foot to quilt stipple, ribbon candy, and free-form cables as described in "Quilting Stipples, Ribbon Candy, and Free-Form Cables" at right.

4 Trim the batting and backing flush with the quilt-top edges. Join the remaining black 2½"-wide strips end to end to make one long strip. (If desired, trim the strips to 2¼" wide.) Bind the quilt edges by hand or machine using the pieced strip.

Quilting Stipples, Ribbon Candy, and Free-Form Cables

Because the background fabric is so dark and busy, it's difficult to see any of the quilting in those areas. Therefore, simple allover stippling in the background is the perfect counterbalance to the more intricate quilting designs that are visible. This quilt is good practice for switching thread colors and tying off threads (see page 12) without being overwhelmed by the task. For best results, choose a darker thread for the background and a lighter thread that will look good in both the lighter fabric and the colorful blocks.

When working with black fabric, a dark gray thread is often easier to see than stark black. Ribbon candy and free-form cables are variations of the designs presented in Dot 'n' Dash on page 51.

1 Quilt a medium- to large-scale stipple in the background around each row of blocks. Quilt a bunch of gently curving lines, making lumps and bumps in all directions. When you get close to each pieced block, carefully free-motion quilt a section of the ditch around the edge of each row as you stipple. This will anchor the quilt as you fill in the background.

2 Continue stipple quilting until the entire background area is filled, quilting off the edge every now and then to check your bobbin level as needed (fig. 1, page 70). Remember to scrunch and smoosh your quilt out of the way, and rotate the quilt as needed to get a better quilting position.

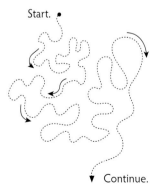

Start.

Continue.

Continuous stipple design

3 Switch to a light-colored thread. Quilt ribbon candy in the block frames, and free-form cables in the colored rectangles **(fig. 2)**. With careful planning, you can quilt an entire row without stopping. Backtrack in the seams as necessary to get to each part of the block. Quilt partial ribbons in the block frames as needed to work your way around the block. Hide the stops and starts in a seam to make them less noticeable.

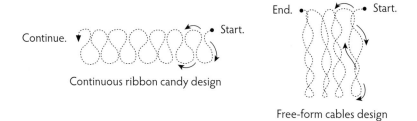

Continuous ribbon candy design

Free-form cables design

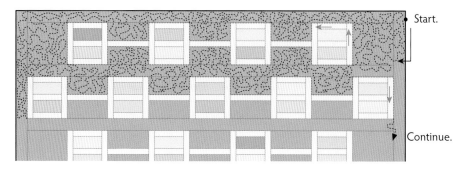

FIG. 1

Background quilting plan

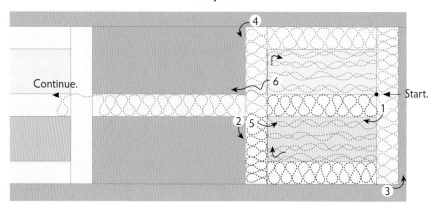

FIG. 2

Block quilting plan

Combined Quilting Techniques

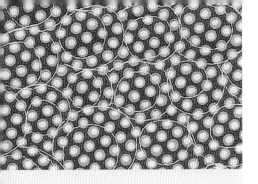

KITES

QUILT DETAILS

- Finished quilt: 96½" × 96½"
- Finished block: 16" × 16"
- Number of blocks: 36
- Batting: Quilters Dream Cotton, Request Loft
- Quilting thread: Aurifil 50-weight in Oyster and Muslin
- Quilting designs: see "Stitching in the Ditch, Double Circles, and Packed Flowers" on page 76

It's hard to believe that this colorful design is made entirely from precuts. Although it's a large quilt, it's simple enough to quilt on a home sewing machine. Most of the cutting has already been done for you, so you can spend less time piecing and more time quilting.

Materials

Yardage is based on 42"-wide fabric unless otherwise noted. For assorted prints, you'll need matching 10", 5", and 2½" squares, so purchase all precuts from the same fabric line.

36 squares, 2½" × 2½", of assorted prints for blocks

36 squares, 5" × 5", of assorted prints for blocks

36 squares, 10" × 10", of assorted prints for blocks

36 squares, 10" × 10", of cream solid for blocks

36 strips, 2½" × 42" *each*, of cream solid for blocks

¾ yard of red print for binding

8¾ yards of fabric for backing

105" × 105" square of batting

Approximately 2,400 yards of cotton thread for machine quilting the print areas

Approximately 2,400 yards of cotton thread for machine quilting the background

Kites is made using three sizes from one fabric line: one each of a Mini Charm (5" squares), Charm Pack (5" squares), and Layer Cake (10" squares) of Summerfest by April Rosenthal; plus two each of Junior Layer Cakes (10" squares) and Junior Jelly Rolls (2½" strips) of Bella Solids Ivory, all from Moda Fabrics.

Cutting

From the cream solid squares, cut:
72 rectangles, 5" × 10"

From *each* of the cream solid strips, cut:
2 rectangles, 2½" × 14½" (72 total)

From the red print, cut:
10 strips, 2¼" × 42"

Making the Blocks

Each block consists of one 2½", one 5", and one 10" square, all from the same print. You'll also need two cream 5" × 10" and two cream 2½" × 14½" rectangles. Although I used one print for each block, you can try mixing them up for a scrappier look. Press all seam allowances open, as indicated by the arrows.

1 Lay out matching print 10" and 5" squares, along with two cream 5" × 10" rectangles. Join into rows. Join the rows to make a unit measuring 14½" square, including the seam allowances. Make 36.

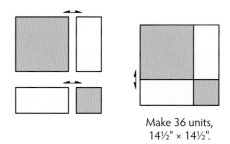

Make 36 units,
14½" × 14½".

2 Lay out a unit from step 1, a matching print 2½" square, and two cream 2½" × 14½" rectangles. Join the pieces into rows. Join the rows to make a block measuring 16½" square, including the seam allowances. Repeat to make a total of 36 blocks.

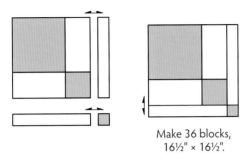

Make 36 blocks,
16½" × 16½".

Assembling the Quilt Top

1 Refer to the quilt assembly diagram below to lay out the blocks in six rows of six blocks each, rotating the blocks in each row and from row to row to form the desired design. See "Alternate Layout," right, for another way to arrange the blocks.

2 Sew the blocks together into rows. Join the rows to complete the quilt top. Press. The quilt top should measure 96½" square, including the seam allowances.

3 Stitch ⅛" from the edges on all four sides to prevent the edge seams from splitting open.

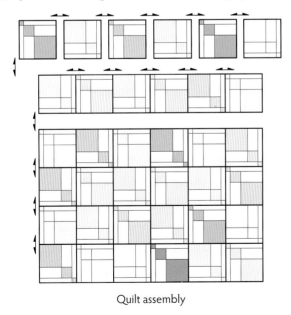

Quilt assembly

ALTERNATE LAYOUT

For a different look, rotate the blocks so that four large squares are touching each other.

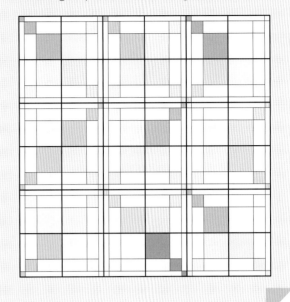

Finishing

You can find more information on piecing the backing, layering, basting, and binding your quilt at ShopMartingale.com/HowtoQuilt. Or for my particular methods, see *Machine Quilting with Style*.

1 Cut the backing yardage into three equal pieces and sew them together to make a backing that's 8" longer and 8" wider than the quilt top.

2 Layer and baste the quilt using your favorite method.

3 Use a walking foot to stitch in the ditch and use a free-motion foot to quilt double circles and packed flowers as described in "Stitching in the Ditch, Double Circles, and Packed Flowers" on page 76.

4 Trim the batting and backing flush with the quilt-top edges. Join the red 2¼"-wide strips end to end to make one long strip. Bind the quilt edges by hand or machine using the pieced strip.

HOW DO I QUILT IT?

Follow this process to easily custom quilt.

1. Stitch in the ditch.

2. Quilt one design in the blocks.

3. Quilt another design in the background.

Stitching in the Ditch, Double Circles, and Packed Flowers

When quilting a large quilt, it's easiest to divide and conquer the task by breaking it down into more manageable portions. Although stitching in the ditch can be a little tedious, it allows you to section off each diagonal row for more decorative free-motion quilting in the blocks and background. When quilting the larger squares with a filler motif, use your fingers to smooth out any bubbles that may form as you quilt. Just be sure to keep your fingers away from the needle for safety. Work your way diagonally across the quilt, following the design of the blocks. Refer to the quilting plan on page 77 to quilt in the sequence outlined below:

1 Using a walking foot, stitch in the ditch on both sides of diagonal rows 1–5, stair-stepping down each row to quilt both vertically and horizontally, as shown in the quilting plan, to anchor the quilt. Rotate the quilt 180° to stitch in the ditch around rows 6–11, working from the opposite direction. It's okay to stitch over a previous line of stitching where the diagonal rows intersect.

2 Switch to a free-motion foot to quilt double circles in each of the print squares in rows 1–11, again rotating the quilt as needed to control the bulk. Travel to each print square by stitching along the seam where the squares intersect. To quilt double circles, quilt a small circle and then another circle surrounding it, backtracking as needed to get to the next one. Every now and then throw in a triple circle when you need to change directions.

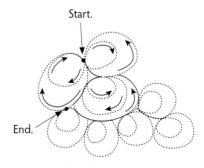

Double circles design

3 Quilt packed flowers in the background areas. For sections A–F, each section can be quilted continuously by stitching through the seam where the sections intersect. Refer to the blue arrows on the quilting plan for stitching direction as you move around the quilt. To quilt packed flowers, start with a center spiral and then echo your way back around the spiral, adding bumps to create textured petals. Continue spiraling around the flower to add more petals to fill in the space. Add another center spiral when it's time to quilt the next flower.

Continuous packed flowers design

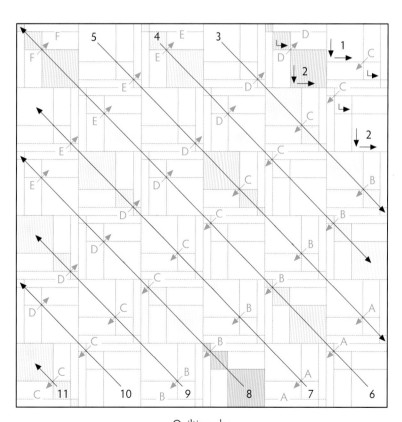

Quilting plan
Black arrows: follow steps 1 and 2 on page 76.
Blue arrows: follow step 3 above.

ARROWS

QUILT DETAILS

- Finished quilt: 78½" × 84½"
- Finished block: 6" × 12"
- Number of blocks: 49
- Batting: Quilters Dream Wool
- Quilting thread: Aurifil 50-weight in Aluminum and Light Avocado
- Quilting designs: see "Quilting Arrowheads and Cursive *Ls*" on page 84

Show off fun and fanciful machine quilting while you spotlight a favorite bundle of colors and light prints in this graphic, modern quilt.

Materials

Yardage is based on 42"-wide fabric. Fat quarters measure approximately 18"×21" and fat eighths measure 9"×21".

24 fat eighths of assorted bright prints for blocks and binding

22 fat quarters of assorted gray prints for blocks

7¼ yards of fabric for backing

87" × 93" piece of batting

Template-making material *OR* Tri Tool and Tri-Mate rulers by EZ Quilting

Approximately 1,200 yards of cotton thread for machine quilting the background area

Approximately 600 yards of cotton thread for machine quilting the colorful triangles

FABRIC SELECTION

Remember that each fabric has two sides! Use the "wrong" side of some of the gray fat quarters to provide more contrast. To cut the fat quarters and fat eighths efficiently, nondirectional fabrics work best for this design.

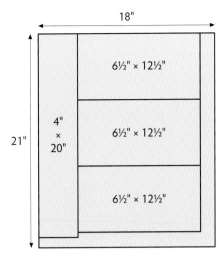

Cutting for 14 gray fat quarters.

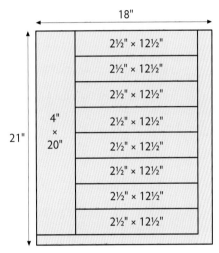

Cutting for 6 gray fat quarters.

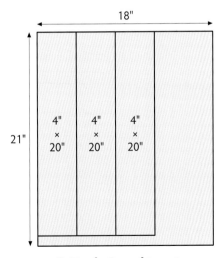

Cutting for 2 gray fat quarters.

Cutting

If you're using specialty rulers to cut the triangles and elongated triangles, refer to "Tri Tool and Tri-Mate Rulers" (page 82) before cutting the pieces. If you're making templates, trace the patterns (pages 86 and 87) onto template-making material and cut them out. Use the templates to cut the pieces. Use the diagrams, left, to efficiently cut the gray fat quarters.

From *each of 12* bright prints, cut:

1 strip, 6½" × 21" (12 total); use the Tri Tool or the triangle template to cut each strip into 4 triangles (48 total)

From *each of 2* of the bright prints, cut:

3 rectangles, 2½" × 12½" (6 total)
1 rectangle, 6½" × 7½" (2 total); use the Tri Tool or the triangle template to cut each rectangle into 1 triangle (2 total)

From *each of 9* of the bright prints, cut:

2 strips, 2½" × 21"; crosscut into 2 rectangles, 2½" × 12½" (18 total)
    Trim the remaining 2½"-wide strips into 2 binding strips, 2¼" × 8½" (18 total)
1 strip, 2¼" × 21" (9 total)

From *1* of the bright prints, cut:

3 strips, 2¼" × 21"

From *each of 14* of the gray prints, cut:

1 strip, 4" × 20" (14 total); use the Tri-Mate ruler or the elongated triangle template to cut each strip into 2 triangles (28 total)
1 strip, 12½" × 21"; crosscut into 3 rectangles, 6½" × 12½" (42 total)

From *each of 6* of the gray prints, cut:

1 strip, 4" × 20" (6 total); use the Tri-Mate ruler or the elongated triangle template to cut each strip into 2 triangles (12 total)
1 strip, 12½" × 20"; crosscut into 8 rectangles, 2½" × 12½" (48 total)

From *each of 2* of the gray prints, cut:

3 strips, 4" × 20" (6 total); use the Tri-Mate ruler or the elongated triangle template to cut each strip into 1 or 2 triangles (10 total)

After cutting, you should have a total of:

50 bright triangles
24 bright rectangles
50 gray triangles
48 gray rectangles, 2½" × 12½"
42 gray rectangles, 6½" × 12½"

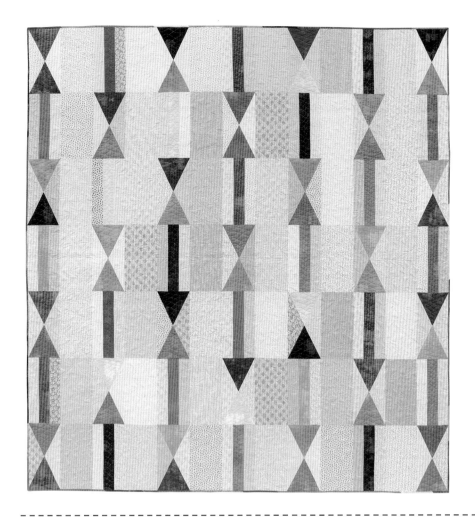

Arrows is made using 22 fat quarters of Behind the Scenes by Jen Kingwell and 24 fat eighths of Grunge by BasicGrey, both from Moda Fabrics.

Making the Blocks

Press all seam allowances open, as indicated by the arrows.

1 Sew a bright triangle to a gray triangle, right sides together and matching the triangle tips and blunted ends. Trim off the triangle tips. Repeat to make the other half of the block using a different bright triangle and a different gray triangle.

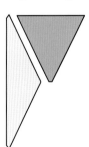 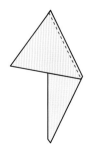 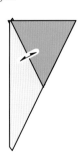

Make 2.

2 Join the block halves to make an elongated Hourglass block. The block should measure 6½" × 12½", including the seam allowances. Make a total of 25 blocks.

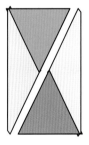 

Hourglass block.
Make 25 blocks, 6½" × 12½".

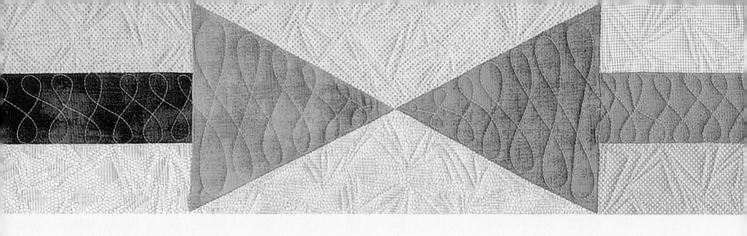

TRI TOOL AND TRI-MATE RULERS

Using the Tri Tool

1 Once the 6½"-wide strips are cut, layer up to four bright strips for quicker cutting.

2 Align the bottom edge (or 6½" line) of the tool with the bottom edge of the 6½"-wide strip. The blunted top of the tool should be aligned with the top edge of the strip. Be sure there is fabric sticking out beyond the left edge of the ruler.

3 Rotary cut along the left edge of the tool to cut the first triangle edge.

4 Rotary cut along the right edge of the tool to release the triangles.

5 Rotate the tool 180° so the 6½" line is now aligned with the top edge of the fabric strip and the diagonal edge is aligned with the last cut.

6 Cut along the right edge of the ruler to release the next set of triangles.

7 Continue rotating the ruler and releasing groups of triangles until you have the number needed.

Using the Tri-Mate Ruler

1 Align the bottom edge (or 3½" line) of the ruler with the bottom edge of a gray 4"-wide strip. Be sure there is fabric sticking out beyond the left edge of the ruler.

2 Rotary cut along the left edge of the ruler to cut the first triangle edge. Move the excess fabric out of the way on your left; trim the bottom left of the fabric along the lower-left blunted edge of the ruler.

3 Rotary cut along the right edge of the ruler to release the triangles. Trim the bottom right of the fabric along the lower-right blunted edge of the ruler.

4 Rotate the ruler 180° so the 3½" line is now aligned with the top edge of the fabric strip and the diagonal edge is aligned with the last cut.

5 Cut along the right edge of the ruler to release the next set of triangles.

6 Continue rotating the ruler and releasing groups of triangles until you have the number needed.

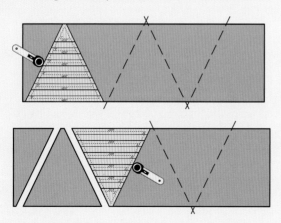

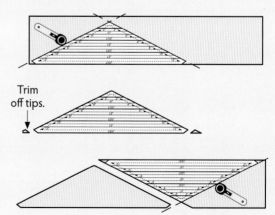

Trim off tips.

PERFECT MATCH

Before sewing the seam, place a pin in the seam intersection in the center of the Hourglass block. Fold back the block to see if the triangle tips will meet at a point. If they don't, slightly adjust the position so that the centers are aligned. You may need to offset the seams by up to ¼" so that they line up properly. Once they're aligned, pin the pieces together on each side of the seam intersection.

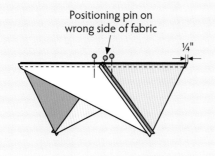

Positioning pin on wrong side of fabric

¼"

3 Sew two gray 2½" × 12½" rectangles to both long sides of a bright 2½" × 12½" rectangle to make a Stick block. The block should measure 6½" × 12½", including the seam allowances. Make a total of 24 blocks.

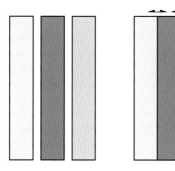

Stick block.
Make 24 blocks, 6½" × 12½".

Assembling the Quilt Top

1 Refer to the quilt assembly diagram below to lay out the blocks and gray 6½" × 12½" rectangles in seven rows. The odd-numbered rows will start and end with an Hourglass block. The even-numbered rows will start and end with a Stick block. Place the gray rectangles between the blocks.

2 Sew the blocks together into seven rows. Join the rows to complete the quilt top. Press all seam allowances open. The quilt top should measure 78½" × 84½", including the seam allowances.

3 Stitch ⅛" from the edges on all four sides to prevent the edge seams from splitting open.

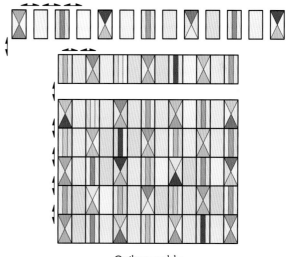

Quilt assembly

Finishing

You can find more information on piecing the backing, layering, basting, and binding your quilt at ShopMartingale.com/HowtoQuilt. Or for my particular methods, see *Machine Quilting with Style*.

1 Cut the backing yardage into three equal lengths and join the lengths along their long edges to make a backing approximately 8" longer and 8" wider than the quilt top.

2 Layer and baste the quilt using your favorite method.

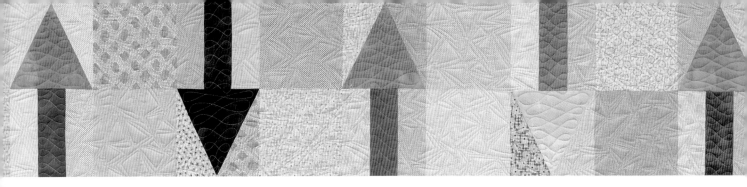

3 Use a walking foot to stitch in the ditch around each of the vertical arrows, following the stitch-in-the-ditch quilting plan on page 85 to anchor the quilt. Then drop the feed dogs and use a free-motion foot to quilt arrowheads and cursive *L*s as described in "Quilting Arrowheads and Cursive *L*s" below.

4 Trim the batting and backing flush with the quilt-top edges. Join the bright 2¼"-wide strips end to end to make a 340"-long strip. Bind the quilt edges by hand or machine using the pieced strip.

Quilting Arrowheads and Cursive Ls

Combine two different free-motion designs to create a custom-quilted look. The graphic motifs shown here are appropriate for modern geometric designs as well as more traditional patterns. By choosing a matching gray thread for the background areas, you can quickly quilt interesting asymmetrical filler motifs without marking.

When quilting on a variety of solid or tonal fabrics, reduce thread buildup by choosing a lighter colored thread and quilting a textural motif that is not too dense. The two designs can be repetitive to quilt, so I recommend quilting only one or two rows per quilting session at a time.

1 Starting your stitches off the quilt, stitch in the ditch around the arrows to anchor the quilt. Work your way across the quilt following lines 1–7 on the stitch-in-the-ditch quilting plan **(fig. 1)**. When you reach the center of the quilt, rotate the quilt 180°. Working from the center to the side, quilt anchor lines 8–14 to secure the quilt. If desired, quilt another set of lines ¼" from the first set of lines, using the

edge of the foot as a guide for line spacing. This will reduce the amount of background quilting needed.

2 Free-motion quilt arrowheads in the gray areas between the Arrow blocks, filling in all of the spaces **(fig. 2, black lines)**. To quilt arrowheads, quilt a smaller triangle and then echo the shape two to three times.

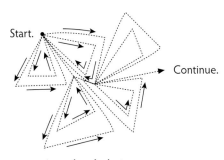

Arrowheads design

3 Quilt cursive *L*s in all of the solid-colored sections, starting at the top of the quilt and working your way vertically down each row **(fig. 2, blue lines)**. Notice that the *L* shape expands or contracts to fill the space. Cross each section of the block at the triangle tips to continue the design.

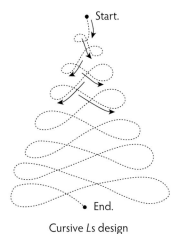

Cursive *L*s design

FIG. 1

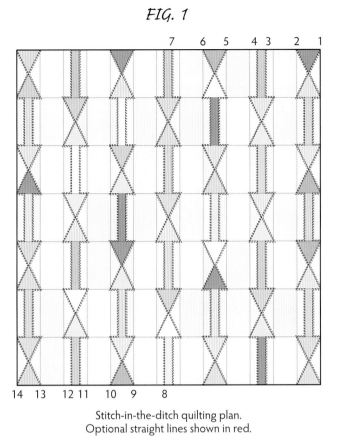

Stitch-in-the-ditch quilting plan.
Optional straight lines shown in red.

FIG. 2

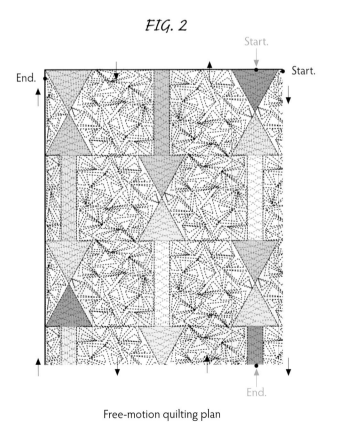

Free-motion quilting plan

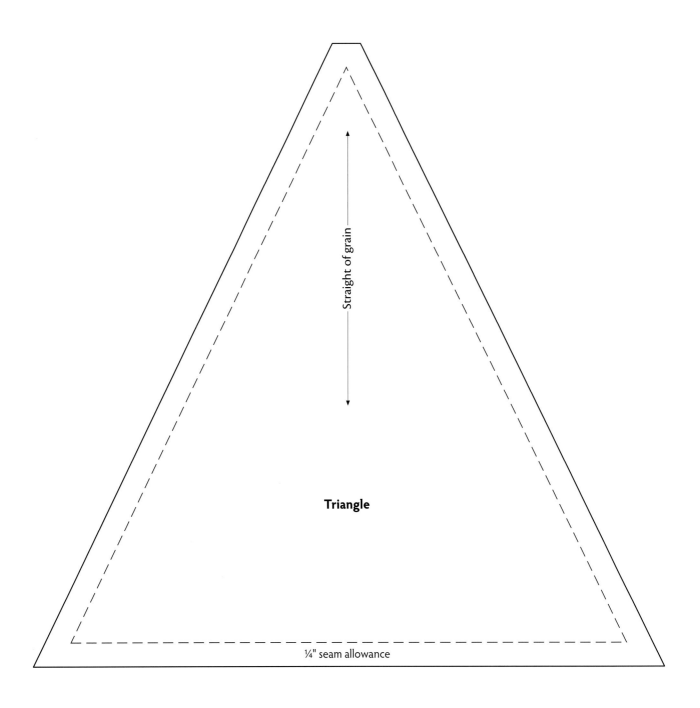

Straight of grain

Triangle

¼" seam allowance

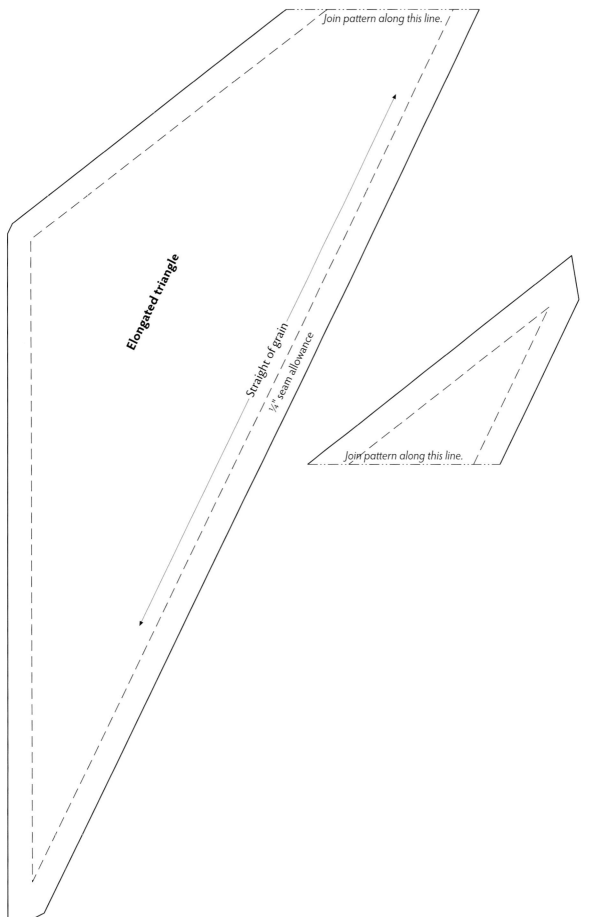

Join pattern along this line.

Elongated triangle

Straight of grain

¼" seam allowance

Join pattern along this line.

SPOOLS

QUILT DETAILS

- Finished quilt: 44½" × 44½"
- Finished block: 12" × 12"
- Number of blocks: 9
- Batting: Pellon Wool
- Quilting thread: Aurifil 50-weight in Bright Pink, Red, Bright Orange, Light Brass, Green Yellow, Light Jade, Medium Delft Blue, Violet, Fuchsia, and Oyster
- Quilting designs: see "Quilting Textured Lines and Free-Motion Improv" on page 94

What do you do when you have leftover precuts you can't bear to discard? Throw them all together in one quilt! Along with improvisational piecing, you'll get to try out free-motion improv quilting in this eye-catching design.

Materials

Yardage is based on 42"-wide fabric unless otherwise noted.

9 fat quarters *total* of assorted medium to dark prints (referred to collectively as "dark") for blocks*

1½ yards *total* of assorted light prints for blocks*

16 squares, 2½" × 2½" *each*, (OR ⅛ yard *total*) of assorted light prints for corner squares

8 strips, 2½" × 42" *each*, (OR ⅔ yard *total*) of assorted light prints for sashing

5 strips, 2½" × 42", (OR ½ yard *total*) of medium to dark prints (referred to collectively as "dark") for binding

2⅞ yards of fabric for backing

51" × 51" square of batting

9 colors of cotton thread, approximately 100 yards *each*, for machine quilting the blocks

Approximately 900 yards of cotton thread for machine quilting the background

Due to the improvisational nature of this quilt, the total amount of fabric you need may vary due to the number of seams and size of leftovers used. The more fabrics you use, the better.

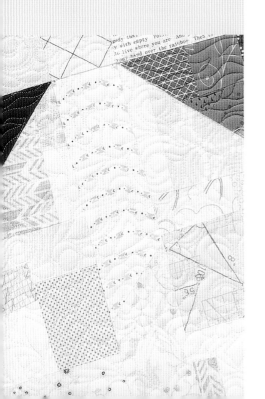

Spools is made using a variety of leftover precuts, including Charm Packs (5" squares), Layer Cakes (10" squares), and Jelly Rolls (2½" strips).

Cutting

The assorted dark prints and light prints will be cut as part of "Making Improvisational Patchwork" at right.

From the assorted light prints for sashing, cut:
24 rectangles, 2½" × 12½"

Making Improvisational Patchwork

It can be overwhelming to sew lots of smaller pieces into enough "yardage" to work with. Therefore, I've made the task easier by creating 5" and 10" improvisational squares to work with. Sort your scraps into color families or mix them all up for a scrappier look. I sorted my scraps into the following nine colors, one for each block: pink, red, orange, yellow, green, aqua, blue, purple, and violet.

1 From the assorted dark prints, cut various-sized strips, squares, rectangles, and chunks of fabric. The pieces don't need to be cut in even sizes or regular shapes; however, use a ruler and rotary cutter to cut all edges straight.

2 Using the pieces from one color family, randomly sew the pieces together into larger units by joining two similar-sized pieces along a straight edge. Add additional pieces along any edge to increase the unit's size. Each time you add a new piece, use a ruler and rotary cutter to trim the unit to create a clean edge. Join shorter units to create larger units that can be joined as needed. To control the bulk, press the seam allowances open as you go.

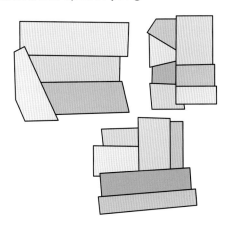

3 Continue in the same manner until your square has grown to approximately the size needed. Don't worry about keeping the edges of your square neat and tidy; the edges will be trimmed down. Make a total of nine dark 10" squares and nine coordinating 5" squares.

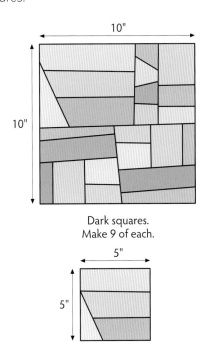

Dark squares.
Make 9 of each.

4 From each of the improvisational 10" squares, cut one 5" square and three 4½" squares. You should now have a total of three 4½" squares and two 5" squares in each color family.

5 Repeat steps 1–3 using light prints to make nine 10" squares.

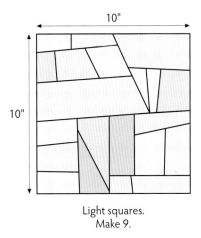

Light squares.
Make 9.

6 From each of the light improvisational squares, cut two 5" squares and two 4½" squares. You should now have 18 light squares of each size.

SPEEDY SEWING

Stack pairs of fabric that are roughly the same size. Sew the stacked pairs together to make a big pile of units before you stop to press and trim. Then repeat, joining pieced units until your fabric is the size you need.

Making the Blocks

Press all seam allowances open, as indicated by the arrows.

1 Layer a light 5" square right sides together with a dark 5" square. Mark a diagonal line from corner to corner on the wrong side of the light square. Sew ¼" from both sides of the marked line. Cut the units apart on the line to make two half-square-triangle

units. Trim the units to measure 4½" square, including the seam allowances. Make a total of 36 half-square-triangle units.

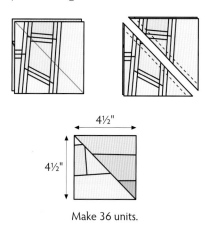

Make 36 units.

2 Lay out four half-square-triangle units, three dark 4½" squares from the same color family as the units, and two light 4½" squares in three rows to form the spool design. Sew the units together into rows. Join the rows to make a block. The block should measure 12½" square, including the seam allowances. Make a total of nine blocks.

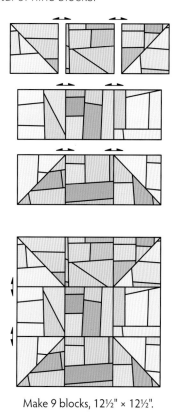

Make 9 blocks, 12½" × 12½".

Assembling the Quilt Top

Press all seam allowances open, as indicated by the arrows.

1 Sew four light 2½" squares and three light 2½" × 12½" strips together, alternating them as shown to make a sashing row. The row should measure 2½" × 44½", including the seam allowances. Make a total of four sashing rows.

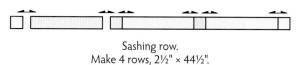

Sashing row.
Make 4 rows, 2½" × 44½".

2 Sew three blocks and four light 2½" × 12½" strips together, alternating them as shown to make a block row. The row should measure 12½" × 44½", including the seam allowances. Make a total of three rows.

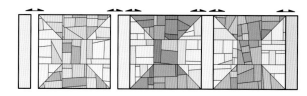

Block row.
Make 3 rows, 12½" × 44½".

3 Refer to the quilt assembly diagram on page 93 to lay out the sashing and block rows. Sew the rows together to complete the quilt top. The quilt top should measure 44½" square, including the seam allowances.

4 Stitch ⅛" from the edges on all four sides to prevent the edge seams from splitting open.

Finishing

You can find more information on piecing the backing, layering, basting, and binding your quilt at ShopMartingale.com/HowtoQuilt. Or for my particular methods, see *Machine Quilting with Style*.

1 Cut the backing yardage into two equal pieces and sew them together to make a backing approximately 6" longer and 6" wider than the quilt top.

2 Layer and baste the quilt using your favorite method.

3 Use a walking foot to stitch in the ditch; then drop the feed dogs and use a free-motion foot to quilt textured lines and improv machine quilting as described in "Quilting Textured Lines and Free-Motion Improv" on page 94.

4 Trim the batting and backing flush with the quilt-top edges. Join the medium 2½"-wide strips end to end to make one long strip. (You can trim the strips to 2¼" wide, if desired.) Bind the quilt edges by hand or machine using the pieced strip.

MAKING RAINBOW BINDING

Select leftover strips that match the colors of the eight blocks around the outside edges of the quilt. Measure the length of binding required to fit the outside edges of the quilt next to each block color. The corner blocks will need twice as much length as those in the middle. You don't need to be exact in the placement. Join the strips end to end using your favorite method and bind as you normally would.

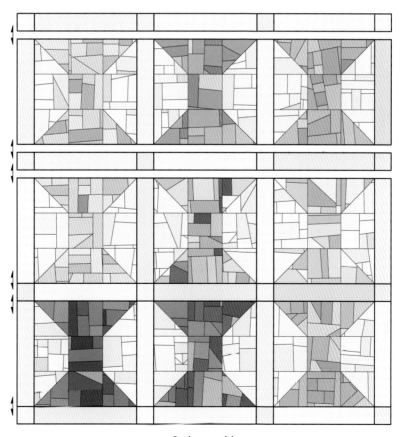

Quilt assembly

Quilting Textured Lines and Free-Motion Improv

In this exercise, you'll become comfortable starting and stopping and switching thread colors in each of the blocks. If you prefer, you can use a variegated multicolored thread and hide your backtracking in the seamlines. Use an invisible thread in the bobbin to avoid bobbin thread changes if desired.

1 Use a walking foot to stitch in the ditch along the block rows, following lines 1–3 on the straight-line quilting plan. When you reach the center, rotate the quilt 180°. Working from the center to the side, quilt lines 4–6 to secure the quilt. To stitch in the ditch along the sashing rows, rotate the quilt 90° and quilt lines 7–9. When you reach the center, rotate the quilt 180° again and quilt lines 10–12. Some of these lines will be crossed over by free-motion quilting, but that's OK as they won't be noticeable. Now the quilt is stabilized for free-motion quilting anywhere on the quilt.

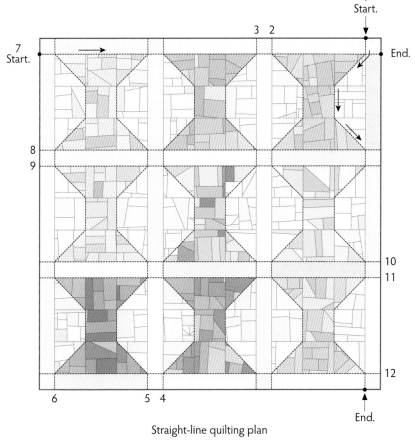

Straight-line quilting plan

2 Drop the feed dogs and use a free-motion foot to quilt textured lines in the blocks. Notice that textured lines is another variation of the wavy line design, one of my favorites! As you quilt the wavy lines, don't stitch from one end point to another. Instead, create gaps in your lines by switching directions as you fill in the space. This makes the quilting much more interesting than solid lines.

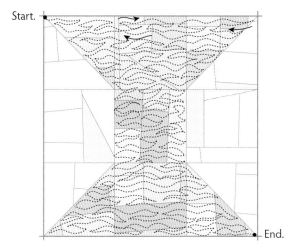

Textured lines quilting design

3 To create free-motion improv quilting in the background, try mixing up your favorite motifs. Quilt two to five iterations of each design, and then switch to another design and repeat. Keep switching motifs and repeating your favorites until the entire space is filled. Try any of the designs listed in this book, plus other free-motion favorites: paisleys, leaves, rainbows, feathers, and more. See my book *The Ultimate Guide to Machine Quilting* for additional quilting motifs.

Free-motion improv design

Acknowledgments

I'd like to thank the following companies for providing products for me to make the quilts in this book:

The Precut Store
ThePrecutStore.com

Aurifil (Thread)
Aurifil.com
All of the threads used to make the quilts in this book can be found in my Piece and Quilt Collection from Aurifil.

Moda Fabrics
UnitedNotions.com

Andover Fabrics
AndoverFabrics.com

Robert Kaufman Fabrics
RobertKaufman.com

Hoffman California Fabrics
HoffmanFabrics.com

Free Spirit Fabrics
FreeSpiritFabrics.com

Hobbs Bonded Fibers
HobbsBatting.com

Quilters Dream Batting
QuiltersDreamBatting.com

Pellon (Batting)
PellonProjects.com

I'd also like to especially thank the entire team at Martingale. After working with them on three books, I can truly say they are some of the best folks in the industry!

ABOUT THE AUTHOR

CHRISTA WATSON is an award-winning quilter, Bernina Ambassador, EQ artist, and author of numerous books, articles, and patterns on piecing and machine quilting. She travels worldwide, encouraging others to experience the joy of machine quilting on a home sewing machine. She loves living in fabulous Las Vegas where she enjoys being a wife to her husband and a mom to her three children, who all think it's normal to have a house full of fabric. Visit her on social media @christaquilts and ChristaQuilts.com, and find her online video classes at Craftsy.com.